1st Edition
First printing
December 2007

Planet wildlife press
1201 W 22nd Street
Cheyenne, WY 82001

USD $19.95

Archery is the NEW Golf

Created by Planet Wildlife

Dedication

To Bryce Michael Maeseele;

Born December 18, 2007.

Our inspiration and driving force.

This book is for you .

"This is the dawning of the age of Sagittarius"

CONTENTS

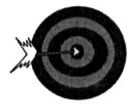

Introduction

There are Archery Ranges and Courses located all over the world. This guide will illustrate locations of Ranges and Courses located in the rocky mountain region, where to pay dues for the range (when applicable) and how to find the range or Course.

There are basically three deferent kinds of ranges:

A. Public Ranges and Courses are usually located on parks or public lands and are free to the public. Donations are usually accepted to help pay for replacement of target materials and other materials.
B. Outdoor club or membership Ranges or Courses will require a fee in most cases.
C. Indoor ranges which almost always require a membership fee.

Although dominated by bow hunters, this industry is experiencing tremendous growth for the sports enthusiast. This sport is relatively inexpensive, sharpens your senses, is a healthy form of exercise, increases mind body unification and is just a heck of a lot of **fun**. Most of our jobs and life creates spinal curvatures by over developing or under developing muscles on one side of our bodies. Shoot a bow for spine alignment! DO not under estimate the value of learning to shoot both left and right handed to make your spine razor straight!

Illustration Left Handed Shooting

Illustration Right Handed Shooting

Archery is one of the oldest arts of ancient times, which is still practiced today. From its first development until the 1500s, the bow was man's constant companion. From 1330 to 1414, English kings banned all other sports because they diverted time from archery and a royal decree of 1363 required all Englishmen to practice archery on Sundays and holidays.

Archery tournaments, as we know them today, can also be traced back to England. Competitions were held as part of community festivals as early as the 17th century.

Whether an experienced tournament shooter, a modern day bow hunter, a hobbyist or a novice we encourage you to experience many **safe** and **fun** outings listed in this book.

Illustration English long bow

Archery Basics

SAFETY FIRST

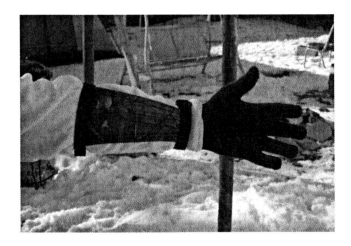

Illustration Wrist Guard

-Never-

Never - "Dry fire your bow" or shoot it without an arrow. This will result in damage to your bow.

Never - Draw, aim, or shoot your bow unless you are sure that the line of fire is clear. Remember, once an arrow is loosed it cannot be recalled.

Never - Expose your bow to extreme heat. Excessive heat, such as your car on a hot day, could lead to limb failure.

-Always-

Always - Check all of your arrow shafts and nocks upon removal from the target. Do not shoot any arrows that show any defects or broken nocks.

Always - Carefully inspect your bow after each use. Be sure all screws are snug and accessories are tight. Inspect your string and cables for wear or damage.

Always - Draw your bow while pointing it at the target. A premature release of the arrow can be very dangerous. If you cannot draw your bow while pointing it at the target without excessive movement, lower the peak weight of your bow until you can draw smoothly and correctly. Over time you will build up strength, and will be able to return to the higher weight.

Always -Draw your bow with an arrow on the string while keeping it pointed in a safe direction. Never draw your bow with a release aid without an arrow. A release aid failure could result in the dry fire of your bow.

Shooting:
Stance Before Shooting:
The shooter sands perpendicular to the target, toes touching an imaginary line to the target, feet shoulder width apart, weight on the balls of the feet. The arrow is laid on the arrow rest.

Extend:
Position your fingers on the string and the arrow between the index and the middle finger. Hold the string while bending the fingers. Do not pull with the elbow but with the shoulders (back muscles) making sure that the limb of the bow remains tightly pulled towards the target without muscle contractions. Place the index finger of the pulling hand under the chin, so that the string touches your chin and your nose. In this position keep the hand holding the bow, the chin and the pulling elbow well aligned in order to have a better stability.

Shooting Stance

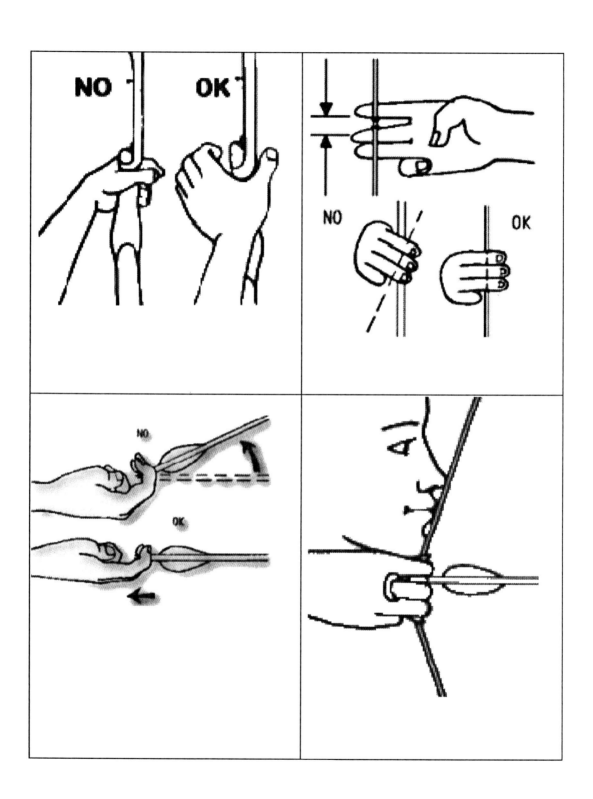

Aiming:

For a right handed archer, aim the target with the right eye through the target viewer.

Release and Follow Through: Bowstring touches the centre of your nose and chin. The fingers pulling the string are slightly extended forward to release the string. The entire body should remain in the same position. Do not change the position of your body after shooting. Excluding the shooting arm, the rest of your body should remain still.

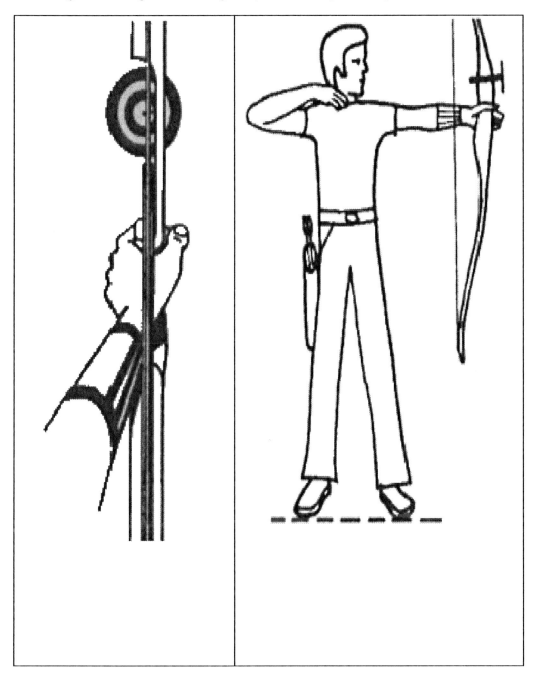

Garden Archery

Build an archery range in your back yard. A good way to start is to open the garage door and shoot at a backstop wall inside the garage Barbeque and garden party shoots and tournaments are WAY fun for family and friends of all ages. Be sure to bring along archery gear and a target when camping you can set up a camp range or carry the target around and create your own ghost course. Cold weather shoots mirror real hunting and survival conditions--- and cold weather exercise cooks off calories in logarithmic numbers!

Illustration winter garden archery 1

Illustration Winter Garden archery 2

Scoring

You take three of your arrows and mark them 1, 2, and 3. When you get to the shooting stake you shoot arrow number 1. If you hit the scoring area you need not shoot another arrow. If you miss the first shot you move up to the next shooting stake and shoot number 2. If you hit the scoring zone there's no need to shoot number 3. If you missed number one and two, move up and shoot number three. The scoring area is divided into two parts, the vital area and non-vital, with a bonus X-ring in the center of the vital area, and scored accordingly. Scoring is based on where you hit with which arrow. The first arrow shot is scored 21, 20 or 18. The second arrow is scored 17, 16 or 14, and the third arrow is scored 13, 12 or 10. The best score per target is 21 and the total possible score for the round, a 588.

Scoring on NFAA courses are identical throughout the US. No matter where you live you can compare your score, your level of proficiency, against an archer shooting in your division and style anywhere else in the country. You always shoot against your competition whether you prefer release, fingers, bowhunting equipment or whatever.

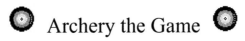 Archery the Game

We at Planet Wildlife believe this can be one of the best sports ever.

The previous scoring is slightly complex for our taste therefore, we suggest "Archery the Game". On the following page is a target that can be easily copied or downloaded in color at www.planetwildlife.net. Scoring for Archery the Game is as follows.

You will see that the target is numbered 1 on the outside ring, 2 on the next ring in and so on to 10 for the bull's eye. Each participant will carry their own target and a pen or pencil. They post their target and shoot one arrow. The scoring is as listed on the target. Striking the bail outside of the rings counts as zero points and missing the bail all together counts as a one point deduction from the participants score. Participants mark their score at the end of each target shoot and add up scores at the end of the shoot.

This target is provided for you by Planet Wildlife to maximize your family fun while playing Archery the Game.

Planet Wildlife is hosting "Archery the Game" on our website and will be posting individual scores. On the website you can enter your scores and the Course or range you were shooting at.

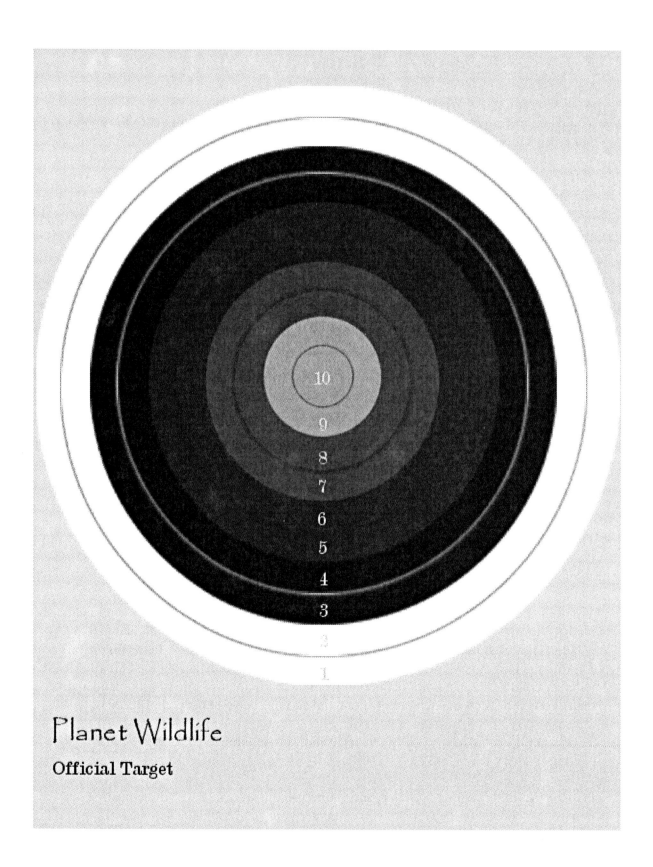

Planet Wildlife

Official Target

www.planetwildlife.net

Listings

Arizona Locations

Colorado Locations

Idaho Locations

Montana Locations

New Mexico Locations

Utah Locations

Wyoming Locations

ARIZONA Locations

- ☐ **Archery Headquarters**
- ☐ **Bear Mountain Sports**
- ☐ **Ben Avery Shooting Facility**
- ☐ **Bull Basin Archery**
- ☐ **Chapman Archery**
- ☐ **Corner Archery**
- ☐ **Desert Archery**
- ☐ **Diamond Point Gun Shop**
- ☐ **Douglas Gun & Rifle**
- ☐ **Four Peaks Archery**
- ☐ **Frank Pearson Archery**
- ☐ **Globe-Miami Gun Club**
- ☐ **Granite Mountain Archers**
- ☐ **Huachuca Mountain Archers & Bowhunters Club**
- ☐ **Lonesome Pine Archery**
- ☐ **Mile High Archery**
- ☐ **Papago FITA Archers**
- ☐ **Papago Park**
- ☐ **PSE Pro Shop**
- ☐ **Robinson Archery Products**
- ☐ **Timber Mesa Archery**
- ☐ **Tonto Rim Sports Club**
- ☐ **Tri City Archers Inc.**
- ☐ **Tucson Mountain Park –TMP Shooting Range**
- ☐ **Usery Mountain Archery Range**

NAME: **Archery Headquarters**
LOCATION: 6401 W Chandler Blvd. Chandler AZ 85226
TYPE: Indoor Store Range
COST: 30 days free use with purchase of equipment. Open Mon. through Sat.
DIRECTIONS: From I10 North or South, take W. Chandler blvd. approx. 1 mile East.
DESCRIPTION: We have a 30 yard indoor range where you can sharpen your skills in the comfort of A/C. We also provide paper racks, tools and bow scales for tuning your own bow. We have the DART interactive video system, you can practices your hunting skills on animals ranging from elk, bear, deer, sheep, Alaskan big game, African big game and one even for kids. If you have never shot the dart you're missing a lot of fun.
CONTACT: 480-961-3100

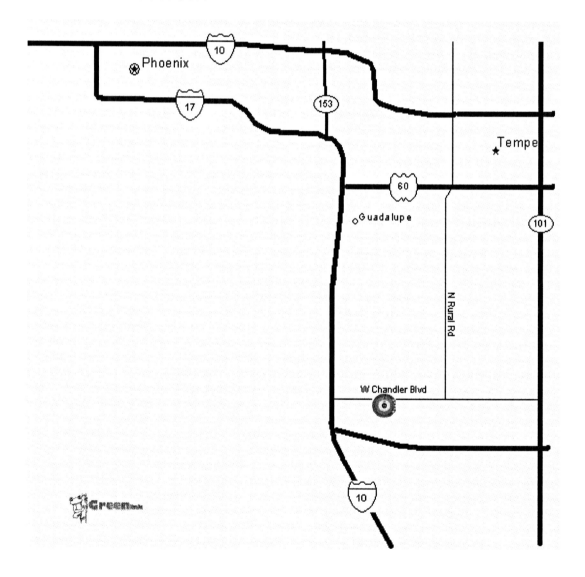

                www.planetwildlife.net

NAME: **Bear Mountain Sports**
LOCATION: 899 E Southern Ave. Mesa AZ 85204-5005
TYPE: Indoor Range
COST: $3.00 per hour or $5.00 per day
DIRECTIONS: From I10 take US-60 East 8.7 miles. Turn Left on S Mesa Dr. for 0.5 miles. Turn Right on E Southern Ave. 0.6 miles.
DESCRIPTION: In store range is 3 lanes at 20 yards.
CONTACT: 480-926-7161 hightower@getnet.net www.bearmountainsports.com

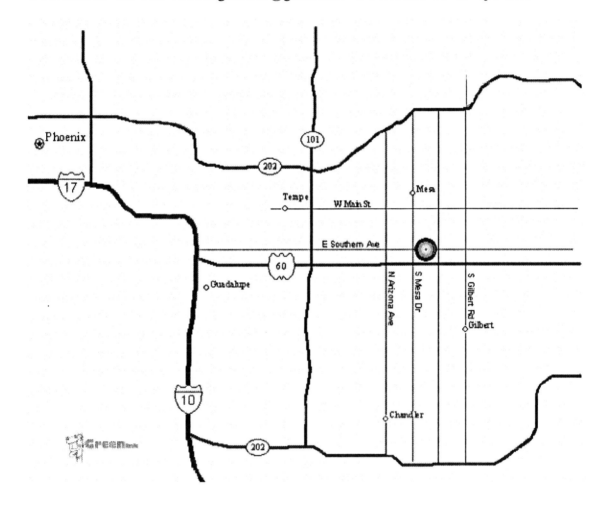

NAME: **Ben Avery Shooting Facility**
LOCATION: 4044 W Black Canyon Blvd. Phoenix AZ 85086-7043
TYPE: Private Outdoor Range (Archery & Gun)
COST: $5.00 per person per day
DIRECTIONS: From I17 take Carefree Hwy/AZ74 West 1.0 miles. Turn Right on N Long Shot Ln. 0.5 miles. Turn Right on W Black Canyon. 0.2 miles.
DESCRIPTION: Facility has a Field Range, Animal Range and Broadhead Range.
CONTACT: 623-582-8313

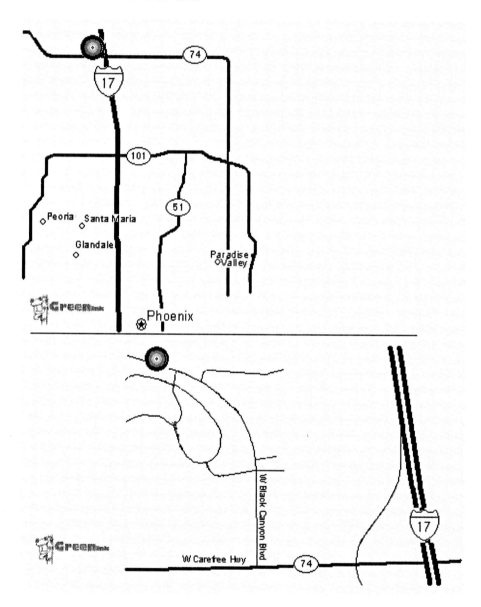

NAME: **Bull Basin Archery**

LOCATION: 2566 E. 7th Ave., Flagstaff, AZ 86004

TYPE: Indoor store range

COST: Free to Customers

DIRECTIONS: From I-40, take Country Club Dr. North and take BL I-40 West 1.6 miles. Turn Right on N Stevens Blvd. 0.1 miles. Turn Left on E Lakin Dr 0.1 miles. E Lakin becomes N Patterson Blvd. 0.1 miles. Stay straight on E 7th Ave. 0.1 miles.

DESCRIPTION: 2 Lanes 30 yards

CONTACT: 928-526-1025

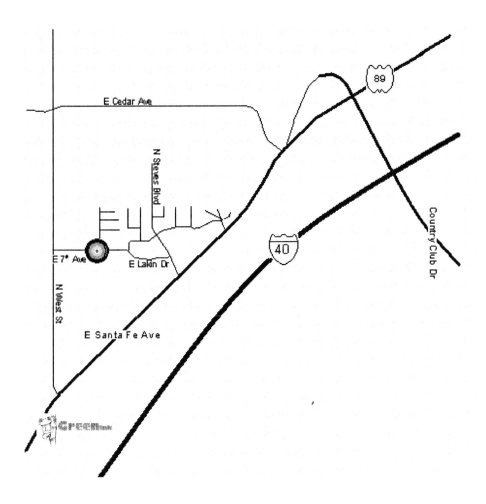

NAME: **Chapman Archery Sales**
LOCATION: 6649 N. Montrose Drive Tucson, AZ 85741
TYPE: Outdoor Range
COST: $6.00/ day shooting, $45/hr school
DIRECTIONS: from E I10 turn East on W. Orange Grove RD. and the turn North on N. Montrose Dr.
DESCRIPTION: Store and School; Range has 2 lanes up to 35 yards.
CONTACT: George Chapman 520-742-5815 www.chapmanarchery.com

NAME: **Corner Archery**
LOCATION: 5008 W Northern Ave, Glendale AZ 85201-1670
TYPE: Indoor Store Range
COST: Free to customers
DIRECTIONS: From I10 North or South, take Northern Ave. 0.5 miles north. Bear Right on W Northern Ave for 5.7 miles.
DESCRIPTION: Small indoor range primarily for customers.
CONTACT: 623-842-3337

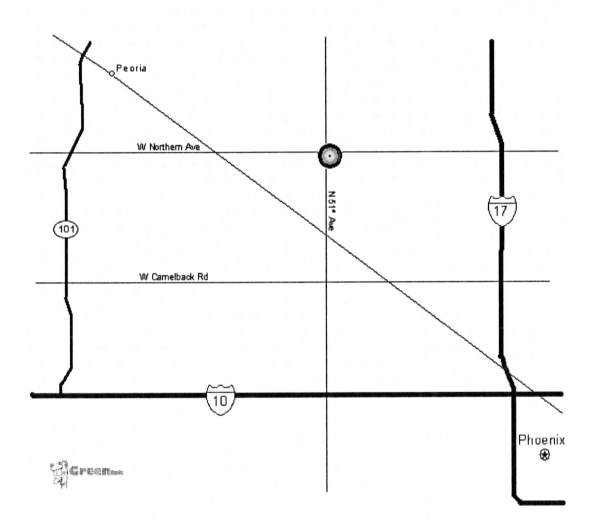

NAME: **Desert Archery**
LOCATION: 4045 N Bank St. Kingman AZ 86409-2712
TYPE: Indoor Range
COST: $5.00 per hour or $9.00 per day
DIRECTIONS: From I40 take Stockton Hill Rd North. Turn Right on Gordon Dr. Turn Left on N Bank Rd.
DESCRIPTION: In store range is 5 lanes at 20 yards.
CONTACT: 928-681-4007

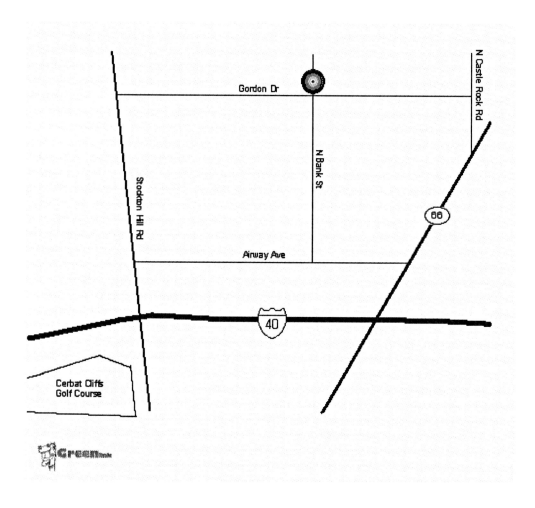

NAME: **Diamond Point Gun Shop**
LOCATION: 788 Pinion Rd. Payson AZ 85541
TYPE: Outdoor Range
COST: Free
DIRECTIONS: From Hwy 87/260 junction travel east 6.0 miles to Pinion Rd.
DESCRIPTION: Range is 10 lanes up to 100 yards
CONTACT: 928-474-5345

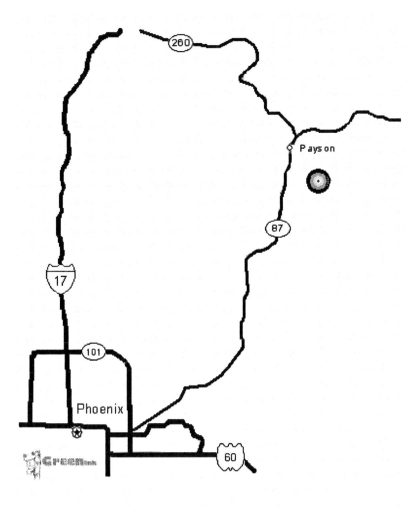

NAME: **Douglas Rifle & Pistol Club**
LOCATION: 3450 Geronimo Trail (PO Box 459) Douglas, AZ 85608
TYPE: Outdoor Range – 12-20 target Course set up for Sunday competitions.
COST: $5.00 public use or for Competitions. Memberships $50 single; $60 Family; $30 Seniors.

The range is open to the public from sun-up to sun-down Wednesday through Sundays **only when a rangemaster is present**. Mondays and Tuesdays the range is closed to the public.

The range is open to DRPC club members 24 hours a day, 365 days a year. Club members who wish to use the range at night are asked to give 48 hours notice to the club so that local law enforcement agencies can be told.

DIRECTIONS: From Douglas take East 15th street which turns into Geronimo Trail at the airport; Range is on the left.

DESCRIPTION: Outdoor range with 20, 50, and 100 yards targets Club also rents archery cubes to patrons. Club sponsors Archery shoot the Last Sunday of every month.

CONTACT: Questions may be directed to Allsafe Security @ 520-805-1970 or to the Rangemaster at 520-805-0293. www.douglasgunclub.org

Douglas Rifle & Pistol Club
3450 Geronimo Trail (PO Box 459) Douglas, AZ 85608

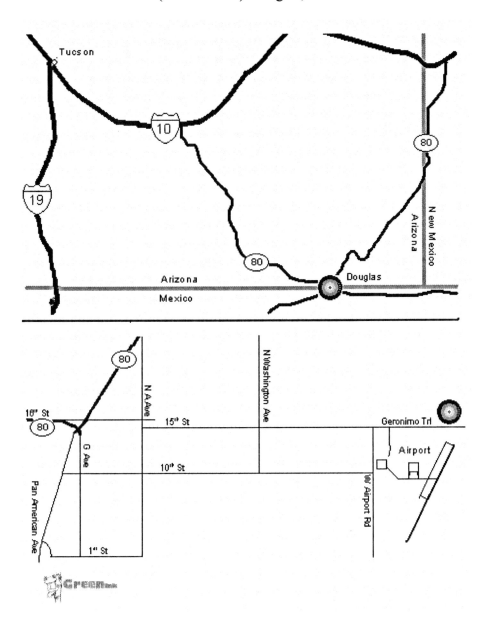

NAME: **Four Peaks Archery**
LOCATION: 229 W Mahoney Ave. Mesa AZ 85207-1254
TYPE: Outdoor Range-Public
COST: $10.00 per Shoot
DIRECTIONS: From I10 take AZ 202 East 12.9 miles. Take N Country Club Dr. South 2.7 miles. Turn Left on W Main St 217 ft. Turn Right on S Morris 384 ft. Turn Left on W Mahoney Ave. 0.1 mile
DESCRIPTION: 25 to 30 yards. This Range Accommodates up to 40 shooters.
CONTACT: 480-834-0958

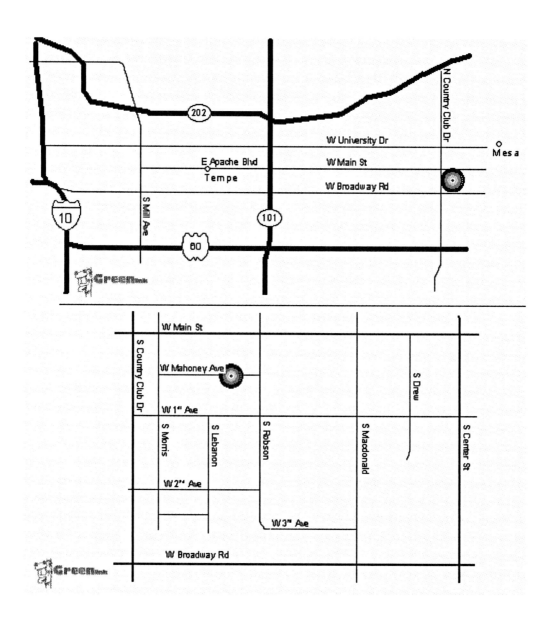

NAME:　　　　**Frank Pearson's School of Archery**
LOCATION:　P.O. Box 308, Saint David, AZ 85630
TYPE:　　　　Private School indoor and outdoor range
COST:　　　　$300 a day; $40 an hour
DIRECTIONS:　The school is located in Vail, AZ approximately 15 miles southeast of Tucson, AZ. Accommodations can be made near the Tucson International Airport. Transportation can be provided to and from the school, if requested.
DESCRIPTION:　Bare Bow – String Walking – Recurve – Compound, fingers or release, for target, 3-D or hunting. Frank teaches all the classes himself. He teaches no more then two people at a time unless you want a larger class. The classes are customized to fit the archer's needs.
Each class begins with a thorough examination of your equipment. Improperly set up equipment could be the cause of a number of problems that archers experience. Improper set up can cause problems with aiming and setting the release off. A lot of times people try to tune their equipment and are unsuccessful just because the draw length is incorrect. You will learn how to set-up and tune your equipment to suit your shooting style and form. If requested, Frank will teach you how to make strings and cables and assemble arrows.
Your form will be reviewed and suggestions will be made to help you improve your form and mental game. Each archer will be filmed so that the shots can be viewed and analyzed by Frank and the archer and later used to create a shot routine for you. You will take home a CD recording of shots you made while at the school.
If interested, Frank will teach you how to learn to judge yardage and how to shoot under adverse conditions such as windy, hilly conditions and pressure.
CONTACT:　520-720-9532 Frank@FrankPearson.com http://www.frankpearson.com/

Frank Pearson's School of Archery
Saint David, AZ 85630

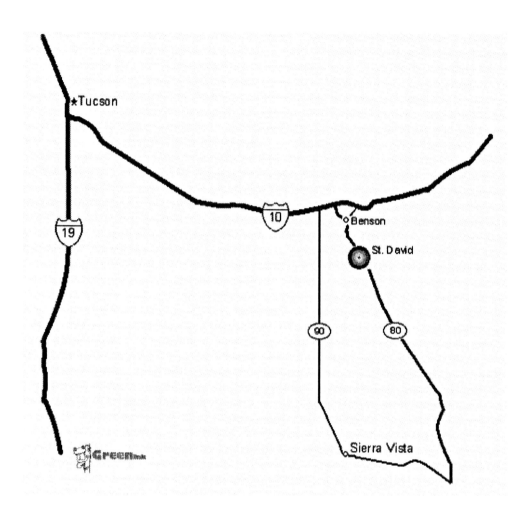

www.planetwildlife.net

NAME: **Globe-Miami Gun Club**
LOCATION: 2675 Bixby Rd. Globe AZ 85501
TYPE: Outdoor Range
COST: Call
DIRECTIONS: Refer to map and call ahead for directions.
DESCRIPTION: Range is 10 lanes at 40 yard.
CONTACT: 928-425-2083/0338

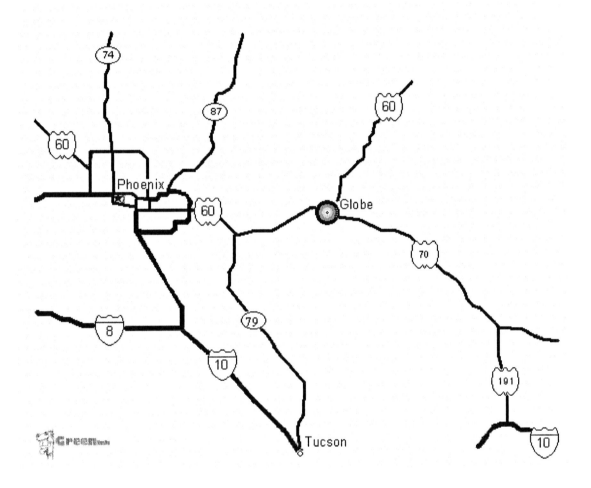

NAME: **Granite Mountain Archers**
LOCATION: Heritage Park, Prescott, AZ
TYPE: Outdoor 3D course and Practice range
COST: The range is to be open to the public on Thursday afternoons from 4:00 pm till dusk and on Sunday afternoons from 1:00 pm till 6:00 pm.
The 3D range, course 2, is intended for members but for $1.00 extra guests can use it. All we ask is one arrow per target, please.
DIRECTIONS: Our range is located in the pines on Willow Creek Road across from Embry Riddle. From Prescott take 89 North. Turn Left on E Willow Lake Creek Rd. Turn Right on Willow Creek Rd. and Turn Right into Park.
DESCRIPTION: There are 72 target butts and an 80 yard practice range.
CONTACT: President Terry Oskerson 9501 Glen Cove Cir., Prescott Valley 86314 445-8510 http://www.granitemountainarchers.com/

Illustration - Granite Mountain Archers

Granite Mountain Archers
Heritage Park, Prescott, AZ

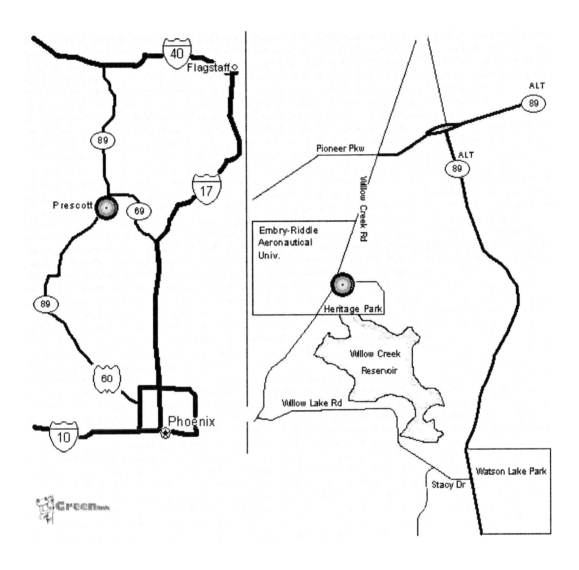

NAME: **Huachuca Mountain Archers & Bowhunters Club**
LOCATION: Sierra Vista AZ
TYPE: Outdoor Range - Private
COST: Membership: Family $20; Individual $15
DIRECTIONS: From I10 take Hwy. 90 South approx. 35 miles.
DESCRIPTION: The Huachuca Mountain Archers and Bow hunters are a local archery club located in Sierra Vista Arizona. The purpose of the club is to foster and promote the responsible enjoyment of archery and bow hunting among all residents of the Sierra Vista / Ft. Huachuca area. Archery safety and good sportsmanship will be stressed, taught, and observed at all times. The club also provides ample opportunity for those members interested in 3D Archery to practice and hone their skills. The Club is a non-profit organization and has no affiliation with the US Military and Ft. Huachuca with the exception that most of the shoots are conducted on Ft. Huachuca.
CONTACT: For more info visit http://www.huachuca-archers.com/

Illustration - Huachuca Mountain Archers & Bowhunters Club

Huachuca Mountain Archers & Bowhunters Club
Sierra Vista AZ

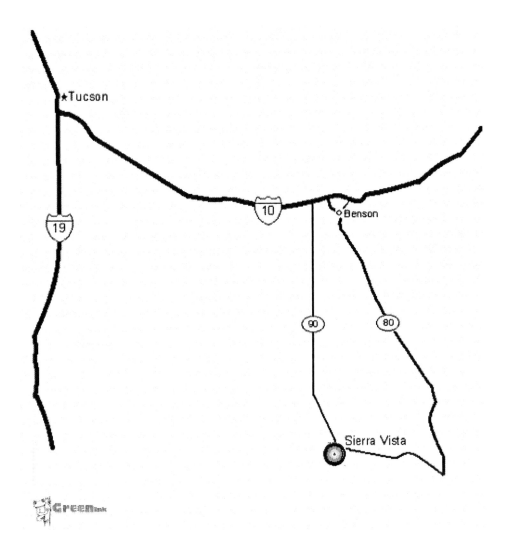

NAME: **Lonesome Pine Archery**
LOCATION: 232 W. Florida St, Holbrook AZ 86025-2544
TYPE: Indoor Store Range
COST: $4.00 per hour
DIRECTIONS: From I40 take N Navajo Blvd. South 0.3 miles and turn Right on W Florida for 0.2 miles.
DESCRIPTION: Ten 20 yard lanes
CONTACT: 928-524-2138

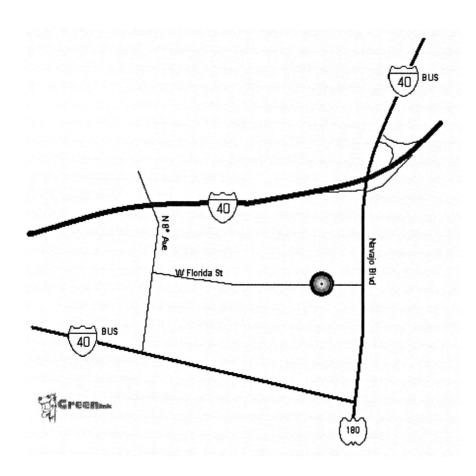

NAME: **Mile High Archery**
LOCATION: 12901 Main St. Humboldt AZ 86329
TYPE: Indoor Range - Public
COST: $7.50 per hour. This includes a paper target.
DIRECTIONS: From I17 take AZ 69 West 16.6 miles. Turn right on Main St.
DESCRIPTION: Open at Noon time Mon. through Sat.
CONTACT: (928)632-5004

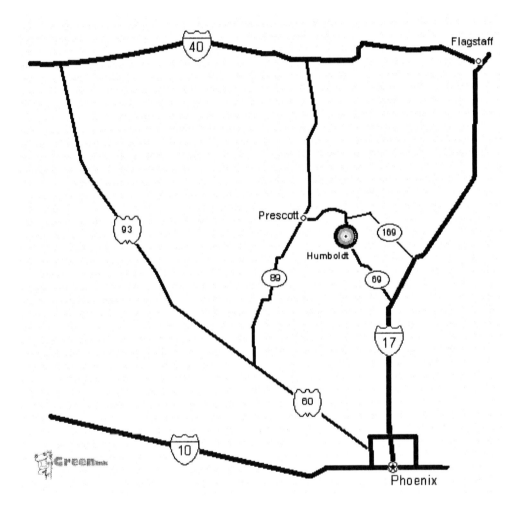

NAME: **Papago FITA Archers**
LOCATION: 6201 E Oak St. Phoenix AZ 85008-3412
TYPE: Outdoor Range
COST: There are no park or range fees and club membership is not required. Donations are accepted.
DIRECTIONS: See next map for general directions. From I10 take 143 North to E McDowell Rd. and turn Right. Turn Left on E 64th St. Turn Left on E Oak St.
DESCRIPTION: The Papago FITA Archers Club is made up of families and individuals who enjoy the sport of Archery. Every Saturday, club members volunteer their time and expertise to teach first time archers the basics of archery. Our Saturday practices are open to all who have an interest in Archery.
If you want to learn how to shoot and don't have your own archery equipment, we can provide everything you need to start. We have NAA Certified instructors to get you started in the right direction. Please go to our PFA Lessons and Programs page for more info.
CONTACT: 480-459-9790

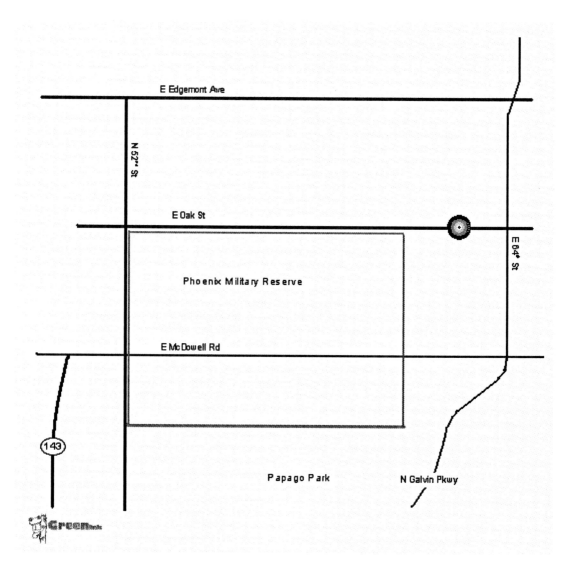

NAME: **Papago Park**

LOCATION: Archery Range in the Papago Sports Complex on the northwest corner of McDowell and 64th Street.-625 N Galvin Pkwy. Phoenix AZ

TYPE: Outdoor Range - Public

COST: $6.00 Park Fee. Open dawn till dusk

DIRECTIONS: From I10 take Hwy. 153 North to E Van Buren St. East to Park.

DESCRIPTION:

CONTACT: Papago Park Ranger Office: 602-261-8318

Papago Park
Papago Sports Complex

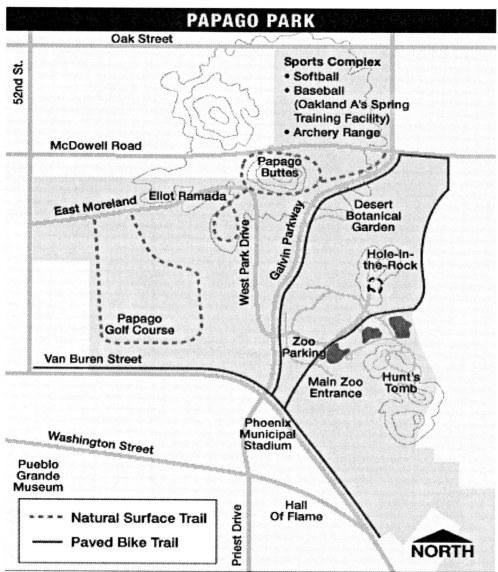

NOTE: The intended purpose of this map is to locate parking areas and trailheads.
The hiking trails are not to scale and should not be used to measure distance.

www.planetwildlife.net

NAME: **PSE Pro Shop**
LOCATION: 2727 N Fairview Ave. Tucson AZ 85705
TYPE: Indoor & Outdoor Range
COST: $5.00 per day; $35.00 per month or $100.00 per year
DIRECTIONS: From I10 take W Miracle Mile Strip East. Turn Right on N Fairview Ave.
DESCRIPTION: Indoor Range is 15 lanes from 5 to 20 yards. Outdoor Range is 15 lanes from 20 to 100 yards.
CONTACT: 520-884-9201

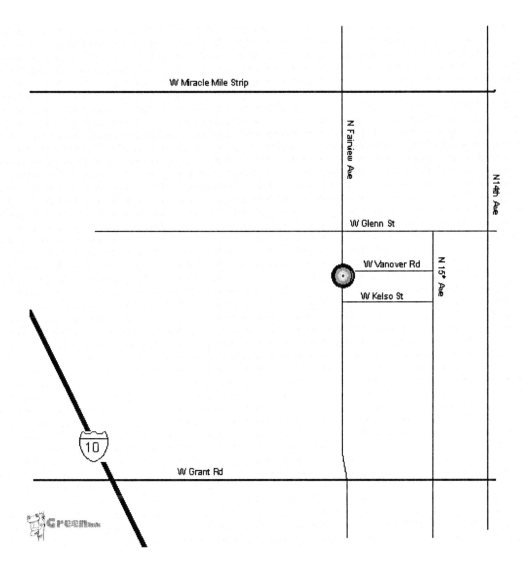

NAME: **Robinson Archery Products**
LOCATION: 8358 E Broadway Blvd. Tucson AZ 85710
TYPE: Indoor Range
COST: $3.00
DIRECTIONS: From I10 take E Broadway Blvd East.
DESCRIPTION: 7 lanes at 20 yard
CONTACT: 520-298-6501

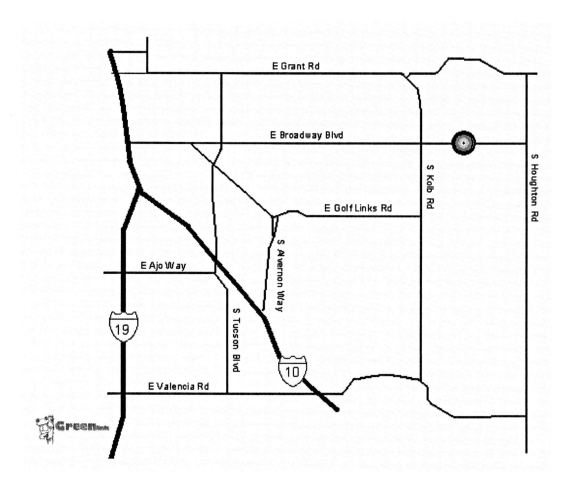

NAME: **Timber Mesa Archery**
LOCATION: 1101 W Hunting, Show Low AZ 85901
TYPE: Indoor Range
COST: Free to customers
DIRECTIONS: From I40 turn South on AZ 77 46 miles. Turn right on US 60 0.6 mile.
Turn Left on N White Mountain Rd. 0.3 mile. Turn Right on E Hunting 0.1 mile.
DESCRIPTION: 20 yard range for customers
CONTACT: 928-537-9808

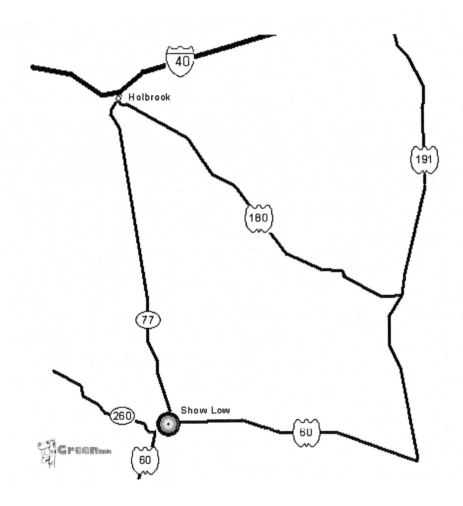

NAME: **Tonto Rim Sports Club**
LOCATION: PO Box 814 Payson AZ 85547
TYPE: Outdoor Range
COST: Annual membership is $35.00 per person
DIRECTIONS: From State Highway 260 turn on to state Highway 87. Continue past rodeo grounds, road to range is located 0.4 miles past mile marker 249.
DESCRIPTION: The Range is open to the Public on Saturdays from 9 AM to 5 PM with a volunteer Range Safety Officer provided by the Tonto Rim Sports Club. The Jim Jones Shooting Range began operation in 1981 under a United States Forest Service Special Use Permit with Gila County. The Range has been developed, maintained, and operated by the Tonto Rim Sports Club under a Letter of Agreement with the County since that date
CONTACT: 602-616-9275   www.tontorimsportsclub.com

Illustration - View of Archery Range

Tonto Rim Sports Club
Payson AZ 85547

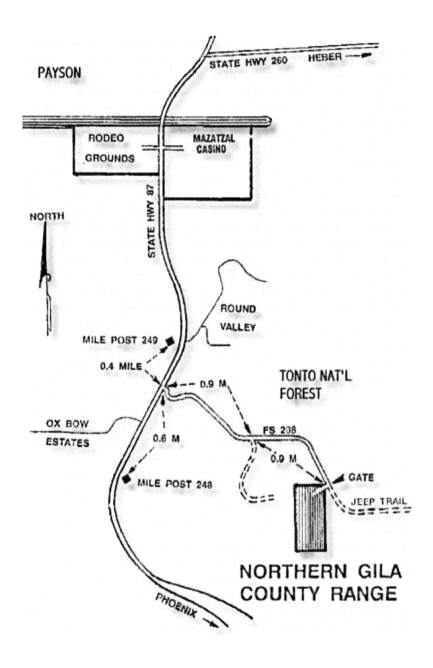

NAME: **Tri City Archers Inc.**
LOCATION: PO Box 432 San Manuel AZ 85631
TYPE: Outdoor Range & Course
COST: Annual membership is $25.00 for an individual and $35.00 for a family.
DIRECTIONS: Just outside San Manuel just two miles from the biosphere. Call for directions.
DESCRIPTION: Range is 20 to 100 yards. There are two 14 target Courses. A large shaded picnic area and restrooms are on the premises. A clubhouse is currently under construction. Property once held a five star rating and club members are working feverishly to reacquire that rating.
CONTACT: 520-403-1369

Illustration – Biosphere II

Tri City Archers Inc.

San Manuel AZ

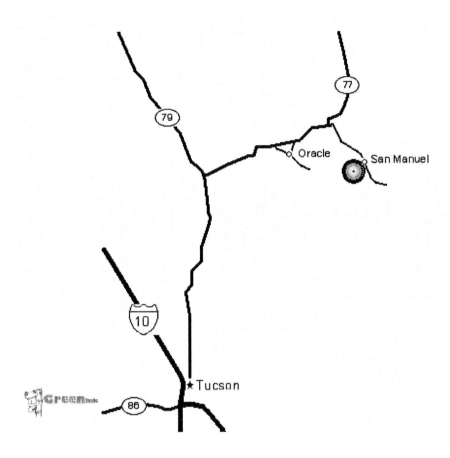

NAME: **Tucson Mountain Park –TMP Shooting Range**
LOCATION: 2200 S Kinney Rd. Nat. Res., 1204 Silverlake, Tucson AZ 85700
TYPE: Outdoor range and course
COST: Daily use fee is $3.00 per person
DIRECTIONS: The Pima County archery range is located in Tucson Mountain Park, one mile north of Old Tucson Studios on Kinney Road.
DESCRIPTION: A self-guided facility consisting of a stationary marked target range and three delineated archery courses winding through the desert. Water and rest rooms are available for your convenience. Open daily 7:30 a.m. until dusk.
CONTACT: Call 877-6036 for information Mon – Fri (park number). This number is NOT a phone at the range.
http://www.tucsonshooting.org/Mt_Park.php

Illustration – Tucson Shooting Range

Tucson Mountain Park Shooting Range

Tucson AZ

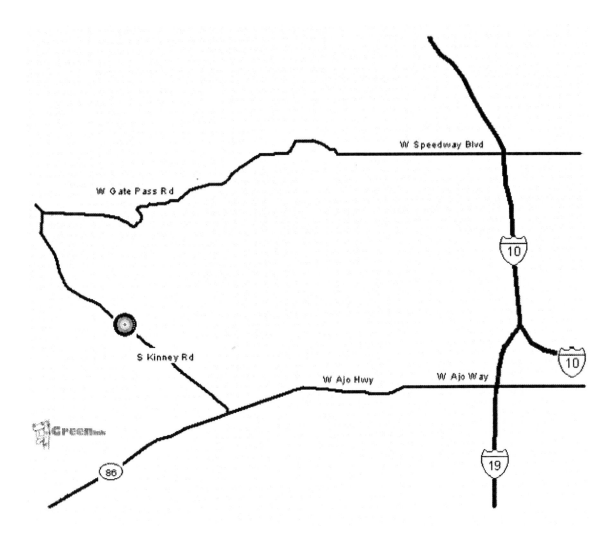

NAME: **Usery Mountain Archery Range**
LOCATION: 3939 North Usery Pass Road, Mesa AZ 85207
TYPE: Public Recreation Area Outdoor Range
COST: $6.00 per vehicle. Open every day at 6:00 A.M. till dark.
DIRECTIONS: From I10, North or South bound, take Hwy 202 East approximately 22 miles. Turn Right onto N Power Road for .5 miles. Turn left onto E McDowell Road for approximately 3 miles. Turn left onto N Usery Pass Road for 1.6 miles.
DESCRIPTION: The only five star archery range in Arizona consists of 100 targets on six separate courses: 17 field practice targets/FITA range: 10 hunter practice targets: 14 field target course, 14 hunter target course: 28 burlap animal target course: 14 three dimensional animal target course: four miles of walking trails: Restroom facilities, picnic areas, and shaded shooting area.
CONTACT: 480-984-0032

Illustration - Usery Mountain Archery Range

Usery Mountain Archery Range
3939 North Usery Pass Road, Mesa AZ 85207

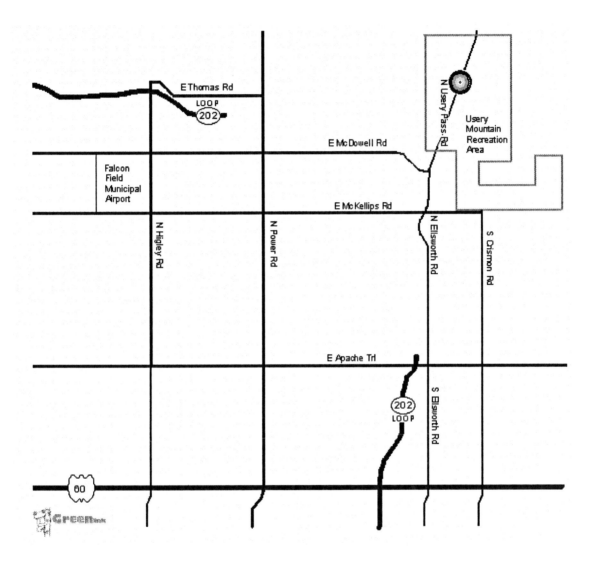

Dave Barnsdale, Winner of 2005 Vegas Tournament says, " without much practice I shot a perfect 300 NFAA round (on Liberty I bow)", "will be hunting this fall with a Liberty"

The *Liberty* I

smaller, lighter, faster

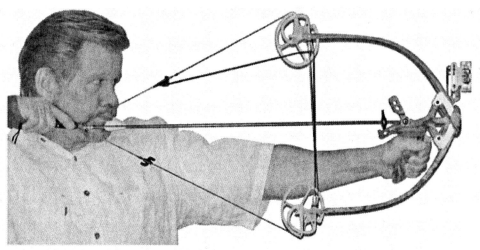

RISER - A357-T6 aluminum riser (same material used for jet impeller blades)

BOW LENGTH - 20.5" axle to axle.
MASS WEIGHT - 2.3 lb. 2.6 lbs loaded with Vital Sight, Peep, and Whisker Biscuit.

DRAW LENGTHS - 26.35", 26.875", 27.375", 27.95", 28.45", 28.81", 29.35", 29.9",
30.5", 31.0", 31.57", 32.0" Left hand bows available.
Draw Length not adjustable. Fine adjustments made with string loop or release.

DRAW WEIGHTS - 40-50#, 50-60#, 60-70#, 70-80# (Adjusts 10 lbs, 2.5 turns)
STABILIZER MOUNT - Center Front (see photo), 5" or less allows fitting in case.
PEEP SIGHT - Due to the string angle special Liberty peeps are needed.
SIGHTS - Only the site head is used to save weight.

CAM - High speed, high let-off, steel adjustable split cable design.
CABLES - 4 aircraft cables adjustable (set screw) 1/2 the weight per cable.
LET-OFF - 85% Hold only 10 lbs at full draw.
BRACE HEIGHT - 7"
AVERAGE ARROW SPEED IBO - 304 fps   AMO - 242 fps

HANDLE: Lightweight cushioned synthetic rubber angled at 29 degrees.
STRING: Pre-stretched (allows for no rubber tube alignment of peeps)
CAMO - RealTree Hardwoods High Definition Green Registered TM Jordon Enterprises.

BOW IS QUIET and virtually SHOCK OR KICK FREE
SILENCER KIT - Sims Super Stealth String Leeches & Bow Jacks Cable silencers

Visit your local Dealer with this brochure to order.
Call 408-983-1127 to order if no Dealer is near.
www.libertyarchery.com Our website with more info.

Liberty I Review
By: **Planet Wildlife**

The first thing we recognized about the Liberty I was that it is amazingly light. When we picked up the bow case we could hardly believe there was a bow inside of it. This is a great asset when traveling, particularly by bus or plane.

The case is considerably smaller than a typical compound bow case. It is about equal to a medium sized piece of luggage in both size and shape. This is easily stored and transported as any other piece of luggage. Although not small enough to be considered for carry-on, it's case is extremely convenient.

When the Liberty I was removed from the case we observed that is approximately half the size of a typical compound bow and again about half the weight; if that, and just as powerful. We found this made the Liberty I very functional in brush or a hide.

We would never consider shooting without proper safety equipment; however the handle on the Liberty I positions your arm out from the bow and bow mechanisms. This increases your personal safety from injury. This bow is more comfortable than any we have shot in the past because of the angled handle coupled with it's lack of weight.

Lastly, this bow gets lots of attention each and every time we take it to a course or range. People are utterly fascinated with the Liberty I's size and sleek appearance. Individuals we have allowed to shoot it are impressed with the power this miraculously compact machine is packing.

Our final conclusion is that the Liberty one is a marvelously innovative design that offers the smallest and lightest attributes of any bow known to us with better accuracy and power of any other compound bow we have shot.

See the Liberty I in action at: http://www.youtube.com/watch?v=-kmF67B3pn0

COLORADO Locations

- ☐ Academy archery club
- ☐ Archery Adventures
- ☐ Archery Hut
- ☐ Arrow Dynamics
- ☐ Aurora Gun Club
- ☐ Baca County Coop Shooting
- ☐ Bear Creek Archery Inc.
- ☐ Bear Creek Lake
- ☐ Bighorn Archery Range
- ☐ Big Thompson Bowhunters
- ☐ Bow Depot
- ☐ Broken Bow Club
- ☐ Broken Spoke Game Ranch
- ☐ Browns Canyon Bow hunters
- ☐ Cedaredge Rod and Gun Club
- ☐ Cherry Creek State Park
- ☐ Colorado Archery
- ☐ Colorado Springs Air Force Academy
- ☐ Columbine Bowmen
- ☐ Eagle County Archery Course
- ☐ FCAA Outdoor Archery Range
- ☐ Golden High Country Archers
- ☐ Greeley Archers Indoor Range
- ☐ Greeley Archers Outdoor Range
- ☐ Iron Rose Archery
- ☐ Lon Hagler Reservoir
- ☐ May Farms
- ☐ Mesa Verde Archers
- ☐ Piedra Bowhunters
- ☐ Pikes Peak Gun Club
- ☐ Pueblo Mountain Park Archery Range
- ☐ Quail Run Sports
- ☐ Red Feather Bowmen
- ☐ Red Rock Archery
- ☐ Rocky Mountain Bowmen's Club
- ☐ Ski and Bow Rack
- ☐ Skyline Archery
- ☐ St. Vrain Archery Club
- ☐ Tanglewood Archery
- ☐ White River Bowmen

NAME: **Academy archery club**

LOCATION: The Academy Archery Club is located in Building 5342 on the ★ in Colorado Springs CO

TYPE: Outdoor Range and Courses

COST: Memberships are available at Grover Cassada and valid for one year from purchase date. Cost is $40 for single membership and $50 for family membership. Daily passes are also available. Every shooter must have a valid range pass prior to shooting.

DIRECTIONS:

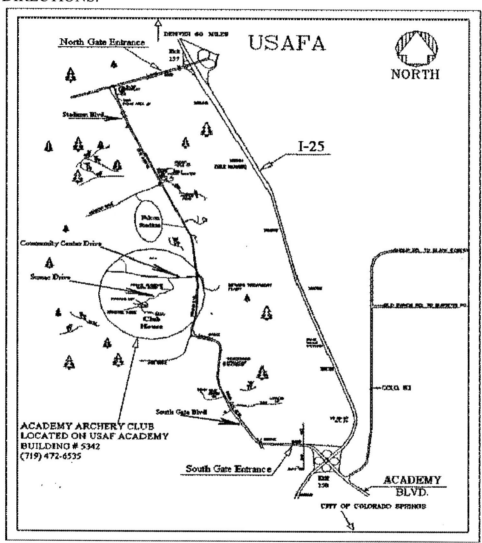

DESCRIPTION: Located on the U.S. Air Force Academy and nestled in the foothills of the Rocky Mountains you will find the Academy Archery Club. Here you can sharpen your shooting skills on our 3-D range or any of our four walking ranges. We also offer a lighted practice range with bales from 10 to 60 yards.

CONTACT: Grover Cassada 719-472-6535

NAME: **Archery Adventures**
LOCATION: 3820 Revere St Suite B, Denver, CO 80239
TYPE: Indoor Range
COST: $7.00 per day or $5.00 per hour with own equipment. With rental equipment $12.00 per hour.
DIRECTIONS: From I70 take exit 281; go south on Peoria turn east on E 39th Ave; turn south on Revere St.
DESCRIPTION: No scores, no standings, Just fun. Range has 30 lanes at 20 yards. Different format each night. Ex: 3-D, 2-D, poker shoot, balloons, dollar shoot , egg shoot, etc. Walk-ins welcome. To sign up or info call. Open Tuesday- Friday 4-9pm.
CONTACT: 303-371-9266 www.archeryadventures.com

Illustration – Archery Adventure Outdoor Range

Illustration – Archery Adventure Indoor Range

Archery Adventures
3820 Revere St Suite B
Denver, CO
80239

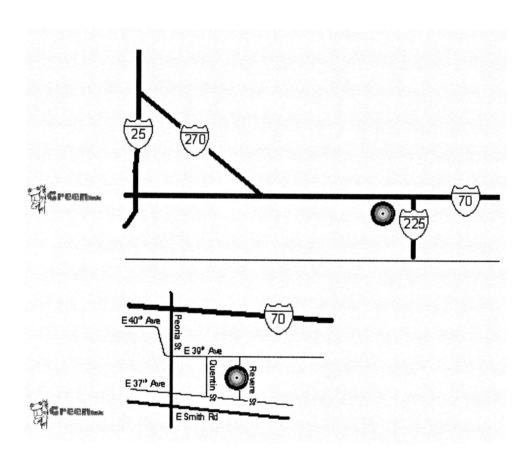

NAME: **Archery Hut**
LOCATION: 895 Ford St. Colorado Springs CO 80915-3713
TYPE: Indoor Range in Store. Open Tue through Sat.
COST: $5.00 all day
DIRECTIONS: From I25 North bound take South Academy Blvd. 4.0 miles. From I25 South bound take North Academy Blvd. 4.5 miles Turn East on E Fountain Blvd. 1.6 miles. Turn Left on S Powers Blvd. 2.8 miles. Turn Left on E Platte Ave. 0.2 mile. Turn Right on Ford St 0.3 mile.
DESCRIPTION: Eighteen 20 yard lanes
CONTACT: 719-638-0554

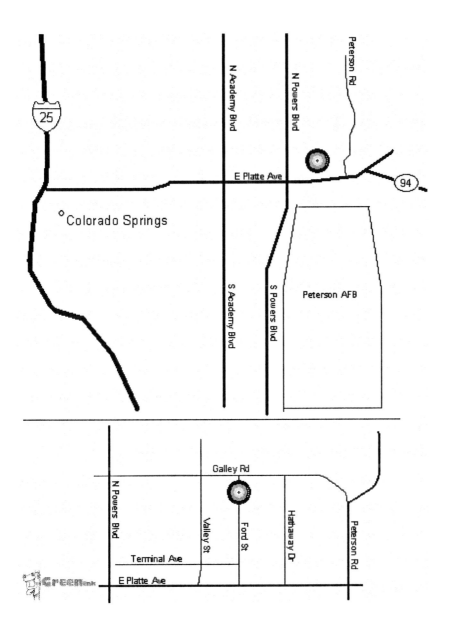

NAME: **Arrow Dynamics**
LOCATION: 2536 Midpoint Dr. Fort Collins, CO 80521
TYPE: Indoor Range
COST: $6.00 with own equipment; $12.00 with rental equipment
DIRECTIONS: From I 25 take exit 268; go West on E Prospect; turn South on Prospect Pkwy; turn East on Midpoint Dr.
DESCRIPTION: 12 lanes 20 yards; Rental Equipment Available
CONTACT: 970-484-4900

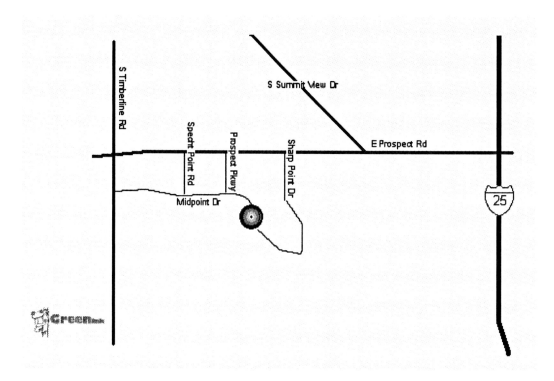

NAME: **Aurora Gun Club**
LOCATION: Gun Club Rd. Aurora, CO 80018
TYPE: Outdoor range
COST: Initiation Fees of $50.00 are one time only. Yearly dues are $150.00.
Note: NRA membership is required to belong to the Aurora Gun Club!
Membership Badges must be worn at all times while on Aurora Gun Club property.
We offer a Work Party Program whereby all members can work off their next year's dues.
DIRECTIONS:
DESCRIPTION: (10, 20, 30, 40, 50, 60 Straw Bales)
Range Hours: Shooting hours are from 7:30 am till legal sunset.
Club House Hours:
Summer Hours (May-November) - Saturday & Sunday; 8 am - 3 pm
Winter Hours (December-April) - Saturday & Sunday; 9 am - 2 pm
CONTACT: Clubhouse phone 303-361-9091 www.auroragunclub.com

Illustration- Aurora Gun Club

Aurora Gun Club

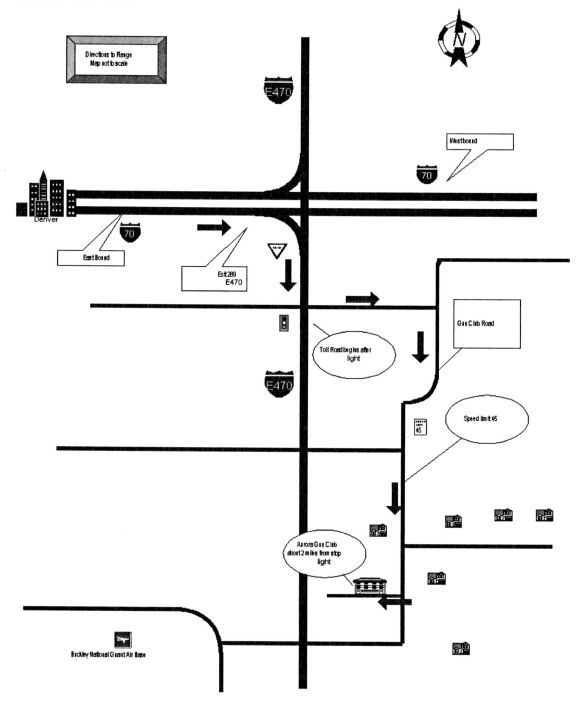

www.planetwildlife.net

NAME: **Baca County Coop Shooting**
LOCATION: County Road W & County Road 19 Springfield, CO 81073
TYPE: Outdoor Range
COST: Free to Public
DIRECTIONS: From I 25 take CO 160 east to Springfield; take County Road 19 south to intersection with County Road W
DESCRIPTION: Outdoor Shooting Range Bring own targets open year round.
CONTACT: 719-523-6591

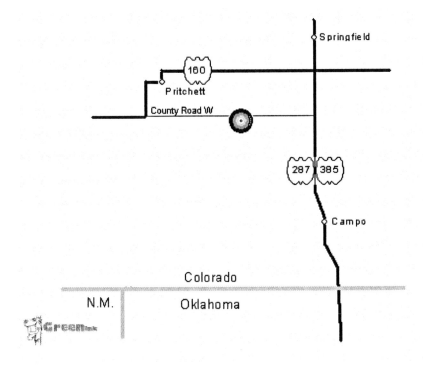

NAME: **Bear Creek Archery Inc.**
LOCATION: 3340 South Knox Ct. Englewood CO 80501
TYPE: Indoor Range and Video Bow Hunt
COST: Range is $7.00 per day. Video is $7.50 per hour and $15.00 per hour from 5-9 PM.
DIRECTIONS: From I15 South bound take US-85 South 3.8 miles. Take US-285 West 1.6 miles. Turn right on S Knox Ct. 0.2 miles. From I15 North bound Take US-285 West 6.1 miles. Turn right on S Knox Ct. 0.2 miles.
DESCRIPTION: Range is 16 lanes at 20 yards.
CONTACT: 303-781-8733

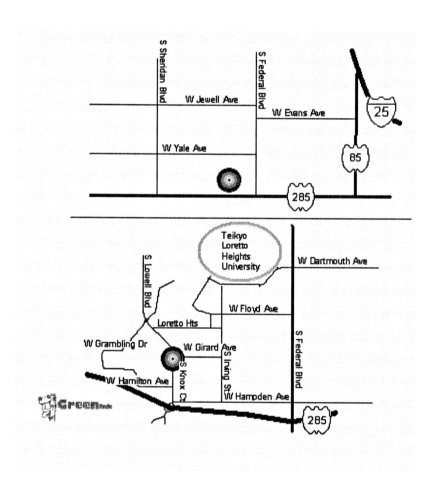

NAME: **Bear Creek Lake**
LOCATION: 14620 Morrison Rd, Lakewood, CO 80226
TYPE: Outdoor Range
COST: Range is free park fee is $5.00 per vehicle
DIRECTIONS: located at Morrison Road and C-470
DESCRIPTION: 12 targets 10-100 yards
CONTACT: 303-697-6159 http:// www.lakewood.org

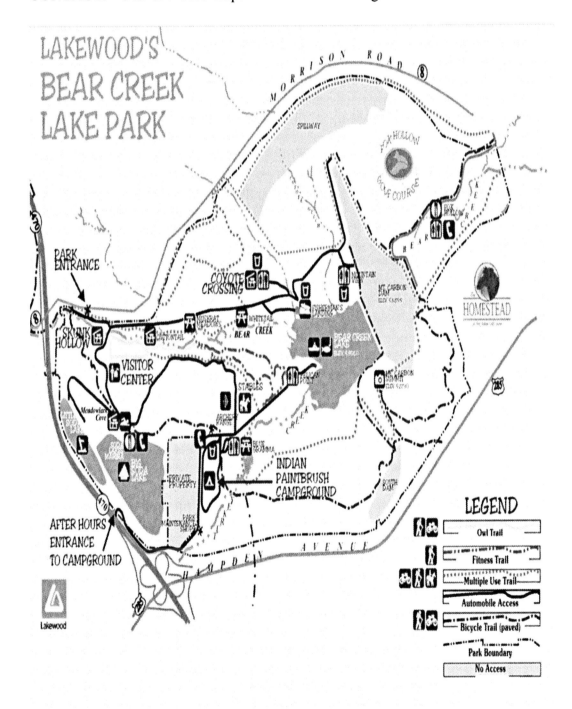

Bear Creek Lake
Lakewood, CO

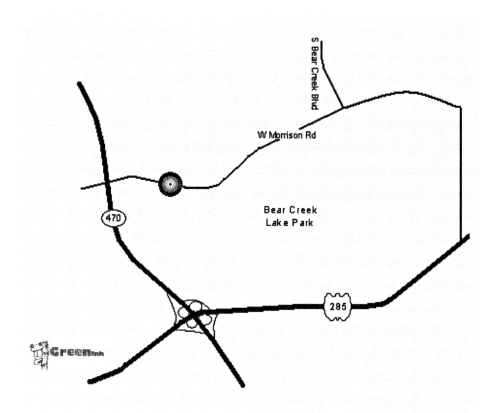

www.planetwildlife.net

NAME: **Bighorn Archery Range**
LOCATION: 600 Reservoir Rd. Pueblo CO 81005
TYPE: Outdoor Range - Public
COST: Free to the public
DIRECTIONS: From I25 take W El Dorado Ave West 1.4 miles. (W El Dorado Ave turns into W Abriendo Ave.) Left on Cleveland St 0.3 miles. Right on Carlile Ave. 0.3 miles. Right on Reservoir Rd. 0.4 miles.
DESCRIPTION: Owned and operated by the Division of Wildlife, the range provides shade shelters at each of its 10 shooting lanes. Yardages range from 10-55 yards. There is also a tower with two levels that is used to simulate tree stand shooting. There are 5 targets available to shoot at from the tower, at random yardages. One of the targets is a 37" steel buck, "Muy Grande" as it's known! The vitals have been "cut out" and archers must shoot through the opening to avoid breaking arrows.
(A Colorado Wildlife Habitat Stamp is required enter the SWA and to use this range.)
CONTACT: (719) 542-6012 or (719) 227-5207

Bighorn Archery Range
600 Reservoir Rd.
Pueblo CO
81005

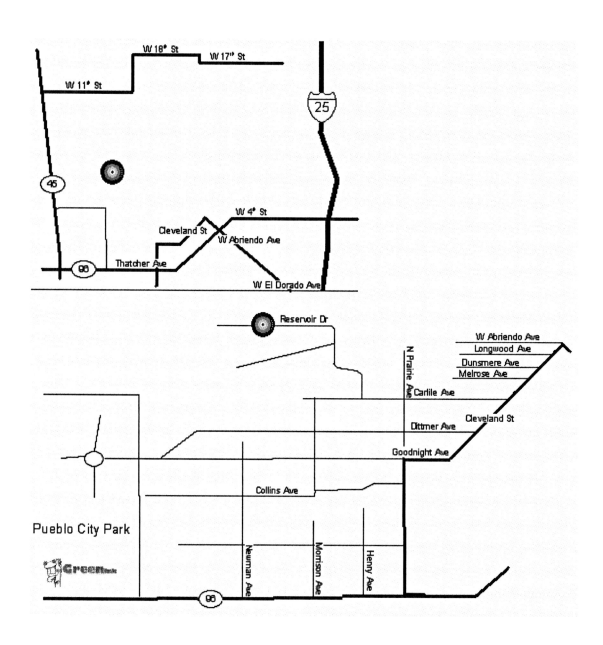

NAME: **Big Thompson Bowhunters**

LOCATION: W County Road 16e, Longmont, CO 80501

TYPE: Outdoor Course

COST: Free to the public with a Habitat Stamp at the reservoir or Annual membership to club is $50.00 per family.

DIRECTIONS: From I25 take Hwy. 14th St SE West approx. 7 miles. Turn Left on Cummings Ave. Take second right on W County Road 16e to end of road.

DESCRIPTION: This club shoots at and maintains the Course at Lon Hagler Reservoir. Excelsior bales. Habitat Stamps can be obtained at WalMarts or anywhere hunting licenses are sold.

CONTACT: Lake 970-472-4460 or Big Thompson Bowhunters who maintain the Course. 970-663-4211 or 970-218-1047 or 303-776-5277

Lon Hagler Reservoir

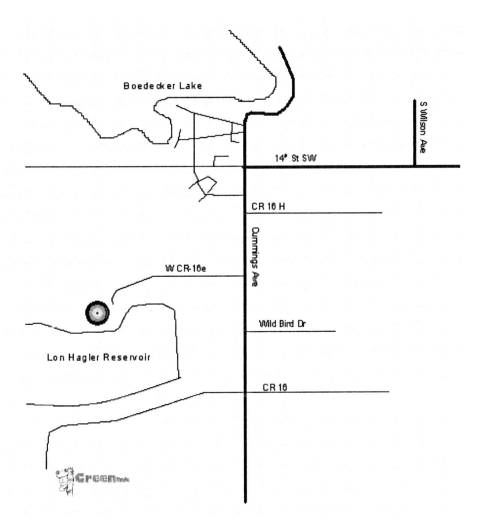

NAME: **Bow Depot**
LOCATION: 2013 1st Ave Unit A, Greeley, CO 80631
TYPE: Indoor Range
COST: $8.00 per day.
DIRECTIONS: From 34 take the business route 34 North to 22nd St. turn east 1 block turn north on 1st Ave.
DESCRIPTION: 18 lanes, 30+ yards; 3D targets
CONTACT: 970-351-8262 www.bowdepot.com

Illustration – Bow Depot Indoor Range

Bow Depot
2013 1st Ave Unit A, Greeley, CO 80631

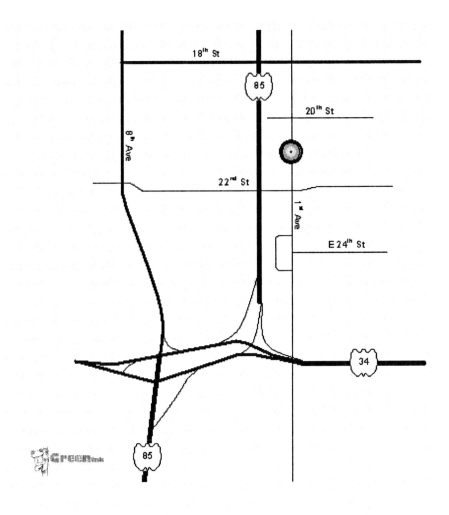

NAME: **Broken Bow Club**
LOCATION: Akron, CO
TYPE: Outdoor Range or Course
COST: $10 per day
DIRECTIONS: Refer to map and call for directions
DESCRIPTION: Range and/or Course is set up and removed about once a month
CONTACT: Rita Campbell 970-345-2511 rita3strings@yahoo.com

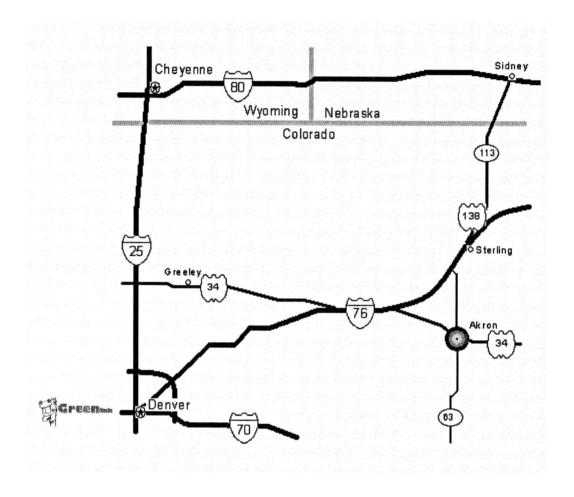

NAME: **Broken Spoke Game Ranch**

LOCATION: 4250 Whitewater Creek Rd., Whitewater, CO 81527-9300

TYPE: Outdoor Course

COST: 3d archery shoots, hunts and competitions

DIRECTIONS: From Grand Junction take US-50 East 9.1 miles. Turn Left on Reeder Mesa Rd. 2.2 miles. Turn Left on Whitewater Creek Rd. 4.2 miles.

DESCRIPTION: Broken Spoke Game Ranch is located just southeast of Grand Junction, Colorado at the foot of the beautiful Grand Mesa in Western Colorado.

Over 2000 private ranch acres with diverse habitat provide excellent hunting opportunities for big game hunting: mule deer, Rocky Mountain elk and black bear drop camp hunts for archery, muzzleloader, and rifle.

Upland game bird hunters will find our strong flight conditioned ring-necked pheasants bright, colorful and exciting to shoot. Field hunts and European style tower hunts provide challenging pheasant hunting opportunities in premium bird habitat.

Your entire family will enjoy our archery 3-D shoots, with 3 course layouts totaling 36 targets in natural settings, trophies, medals, door prizes, and divisions for all skill levels.

CONTACT: Cliff and Judy Davis 970-241-3949 www.brokenspokeranch.com

Broken Spoke Game Ranch
4250 Whitewater Creek Rd
Whitewater, CO 81527-9300

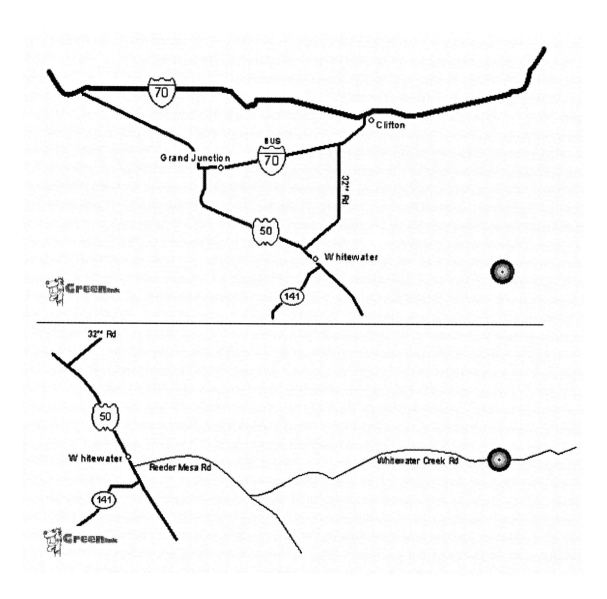

www.planetwildlife.net

NAME: **Browns Canyon Bow hunters**
LOCATION: Salida, CO
TYPE: Outdoor Course
COST: Club memberships are available from Don Palmer at Western Recreation Industries or Roy Abbott at Hylton Lumber and valid from January to December. Cost is $10.00 per family and $5.00 for single membership. A family is one or two adults and children under 18 years old.
DIRECTIONS: The Chaffee County public range is located 9.7 miles North of Poncha Springs, Colorado on Highway 50.
DESCRIPTION: Excelsior bails.
CONTACT: Rick Dissmeyer 719-539-1490 www.brownscanyonbowhunters.com

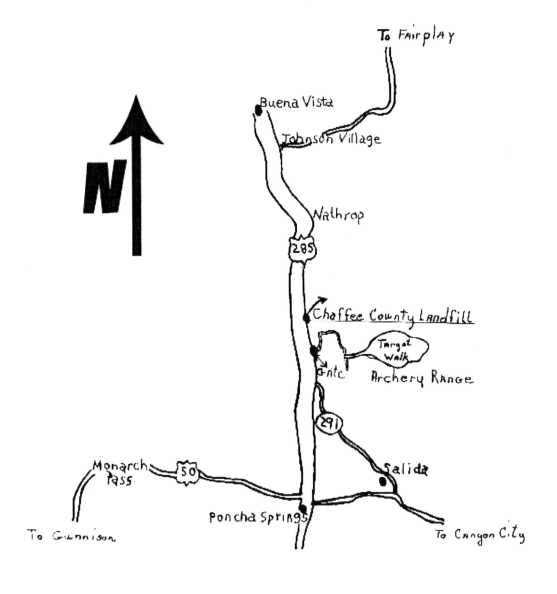

NAME: **Cedaredge Rod and Gun Club**
LOCATION: 1800 R75 Road, Cedaredge, CO
TYPE: Outdoor Course
COST: Annual Membership $30.00 year
DIRECTIONS: From CO 65 take NW Sagebrush Ave west; turn south on NW 9th st; turn west on R75 Lane.
DESCRIPTION: 13 target outdoor course with 3D targets
CONTACT: Todd Fairchild Club president 970-856-1065

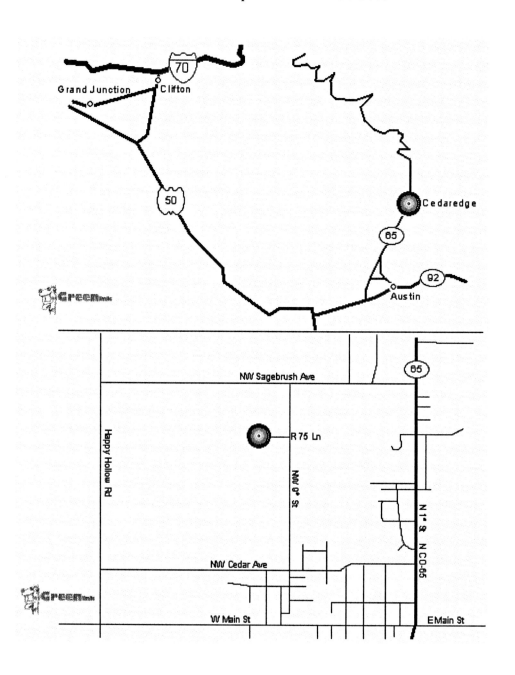

www.planetwildlife.net

NAME: **Family Shooting Center at Cherry Creek State Park**
LOCATION: The Family Shooting Center is located in Cherry Creek State Park.
                4201 South Parker Road Aurora, CO 80014
TYPE: Outdoor Range
COST: A state parks pass is required for entrance. Standard Range Fee (per shooter per day): $13.00 - adult, $11.00 - military/police, $9.00 - youth (under 18), and $9.00 - seniors (65 and older)
DIRECTIONS: East Entrance: Located at Lehigh Ave. & Parker Rd. (3800 S. Parker Rd.). West Entrance: Located at Union & Dayton. (4700 S. Dayton). Please Note: If the park is at high capacity, use the West entrance to avoid the line of vehicles waiting to enter.
DESCRIPTION: a full service public outdoor range offering pistol shooting, rifle shooting at 50 yards and 100 yards, shotgun shooting and archery. Open 7 days a week (some holidays excluded / weather permitting). Hours of operation are:
10:00 AM - 5:30 PM Monday - Friday,   9:00 AM - 5:30 PM Saturday and Sunday
CONTACT: 303-680-5401 http://www.familyshootingcenter.com/
 Park http://parks.state.co.us/Parks/CherryCreek/

Illustration- deer at Cherry Creek

NAME: **Colorado Archery**
LOCATION: 12305 N Dumont Way Unit A, Littleton, CO
TYPE: Indoor Range
COST: $8.00 per day with own equipment; $10.00 a day with rental equipment.
DIRECTIONS: Just west of the intersection at Santa Fe and Highlands Ranch Parkway
DESCRIPTION: 18 indoor lanes 18 meter and 20 yard marked shooting lines
CONTACT: 303-346-9214 www.coloradoarchery.com

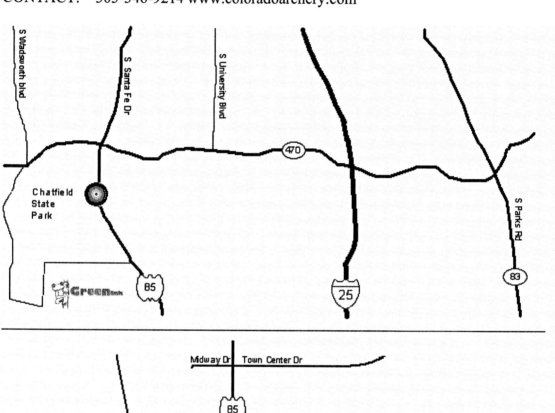

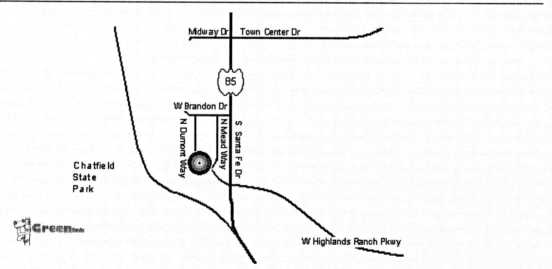

NAME: **Colorado Springs Air Force Academy**
LOCATION: Colorado Springs, CO
TYPE: Course and Range
COST: Call
DIRECTIONS: Go to Air force Academy south gate, to Community Center Dr. turn left to Sumac DR. Turn Left on Sumac follow signs to Archery Course.
DESCRIPTION: Clubhouse opens 10:00 am to dark Tuesday and Saturday Excelsior Bales and 3D targets. 20 3D targets available. Course consists of 56 bales on 240 acres.
CONTACT: Doug 719-333-3557 cell 719-271-0841

Illustration Garden of the Gods

Colorado Springs Air Force Academy
Colorado Springs, CO

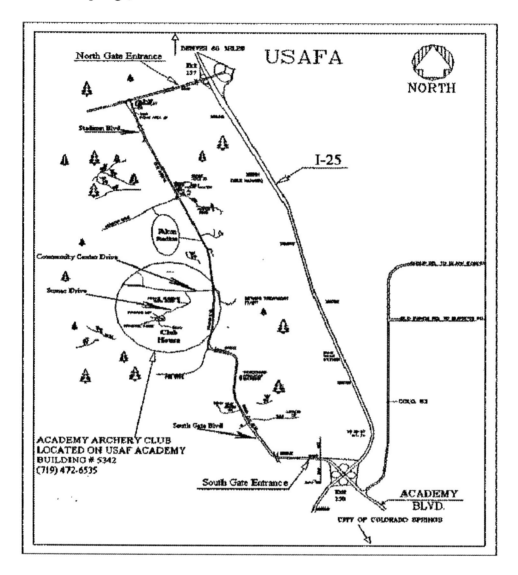

NAME: **Columbine Bowmen**
LOCATION: 159 state highway 67 west, Sedalia, CO 80135
TYPE: Outdoor Range
COST: Annual club membership: Single $65.00; Family 80.00
DIRECTIONS: From Sedalia take Hwy 67 west; turn north at the red mailbox onto the forest service dirt road to the range.
DESCRIPTION: 28 targets
CONTACT: 303-840-3856 http://www.columbinebowmen.org/index.html

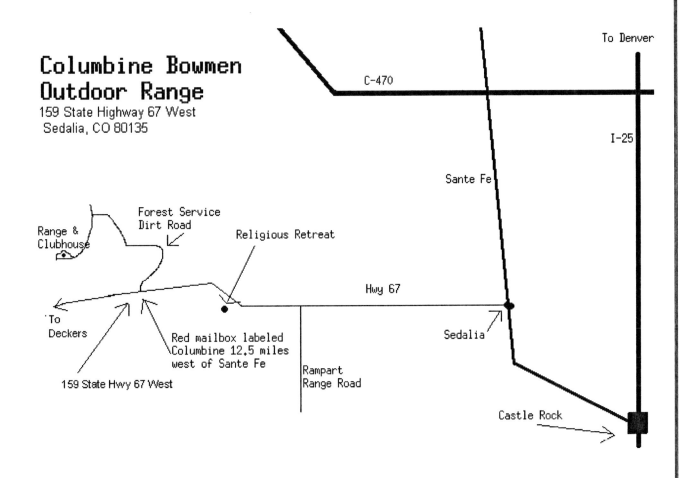

NAME: **Eagle County Archery Course**
LOCATION: Salida CO
TYPE: Outdoor Range and Course
COST: FREE to the public
DIRECTIONS: 3.5 miles North of US50 & US 285 interchange on US 286 on same exit as Sanitary Landfill
DESCRIPTION: there is a good parking area, toilets a barbeque and table for picnics. For the most part the course is a leisurely walk among scented pine forests with well thought out varied target opportunities on excelsior bails. The hills roll so there is a little climbing, but nothing rigorous. In every direction are towering views of snow caped peaks!
CONTACT: None

Illustration Salida Course 1

Illustration Salida Course 2

Illustration: Salida Course 3

Eagle County Archery Course
Salida CO

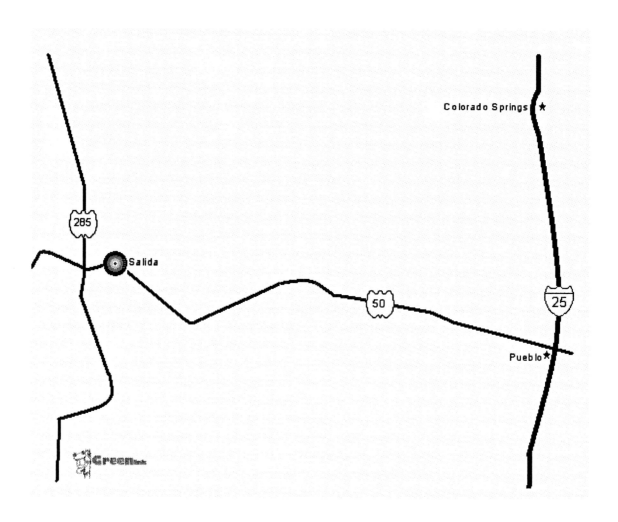

NAME: **FCAA Outdoor Archery Range**
LOCATION: I25 Frontage Road East Fort Collins CO
TYPE: Public Outdoor Range
COST: **Free to the public**
DIRECTIONS: From I25 North or South, exit on E. Prospect Road and proceed west. Turn Left (South) on SW Frontage Road and keep to the Left. Follow Road to its end.
DESCRIPTION: Great parking good restrooms and large covered gazebo with picnic tables and barbeque   Thirty one lane targets are available for practice shooting. The course consists of Eighteen targets all laid out along a forested waterway. The walk is more leisurely than challenging. There are many developments, blinds to shoot from tree stands, stream side cobbled walks under weeping willows interesting and scenic shots across ponds and wet lands at unmarked distances on a walk-around trail which feature burlap on excelsior bails with outlines of various game animals. Nine are standard practice targets at measured distances from 10 to 50 yards and four are on the FITA range at 30, 50, 70 and 90 meters. Blunts and broad heads are not allowed on the practice targets but may be used at the broad head pit, a separate section of the range with a sand backstop. The course is all laid out on a beautiful western river front habitat many wild animals frequent the area.
CONTACT: Membership Director: Marci Riddle (970) 686-9968

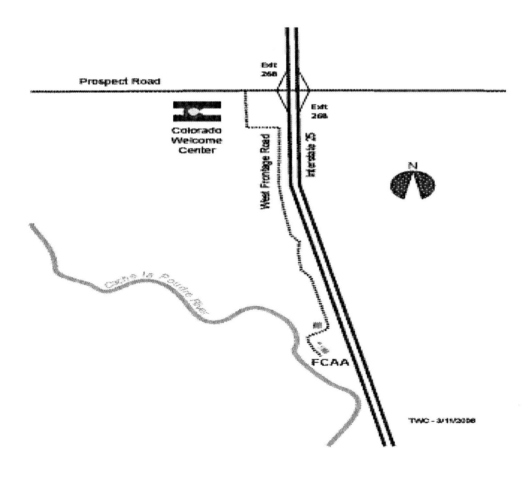

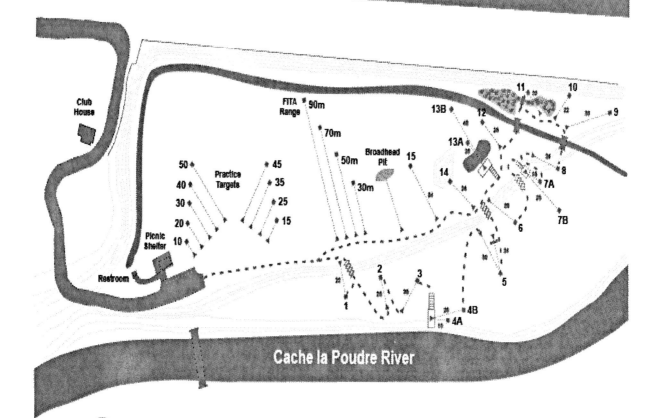

Fort Collins Archery Association
Archery Range

NAME: **Golden High Country Archers**
LOCATION: PO Box 16484 Golden, CO 80402
TYPE: Outdoor Range and Course
COST: New Member Initiation Fee $75; Renewal Work Party Fee (if applicable) $75
Individual Membership Dues $40; Family Membership Dues $50 (Includes spouse & children 18 & under)
DIRECTIONS: Coming from the East, on I-70 exit the Highway 58 exit to Golden, Take the McIntyre Street exit and go North. At the first light turn Left (West) and drive on 44th St. until you cross the railroad tracks. The next street to the North after the tracks is Salvia St. Turn right (North) and follow it to the parking lot by the ball fields, park in the first lot. DO NOT drive back to the range if gate is open on west side of lot! The Archery Range is across the ball park in the North West corner of the complex.
From the West from Golden, get on 44th St. and head east, After you pass the Train Museum, the next street is Salvia St. turn left (North) follow it also to the ball field parking lot and Park as before.
DESCRIPTION: 20 station 3D target course
CONTACT: 303-427-9179 www.goldenhighcountryarchers.org

Illustration – Golden High Country Archers 3D Range

Golden High Country Archers
Golden, CO 80402

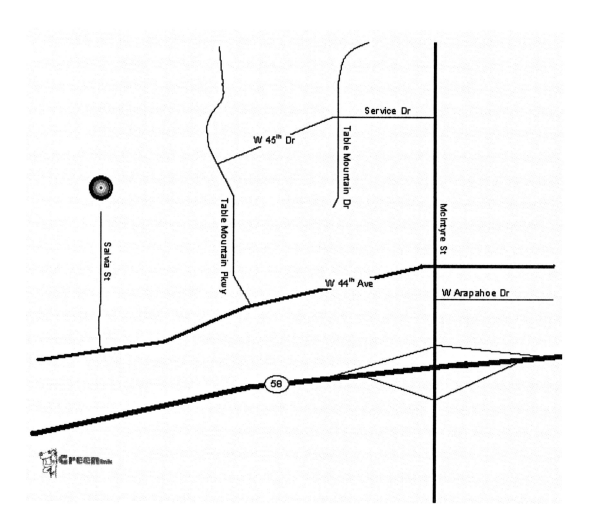

NAME: **Greeley Archers Indoor Range & Greeley Archers Outdoor Range**
LOCATION: 651 10th Avenue, Greeley CO   42nd St & Belmont Ave, Evans CO
TYPE: Public Indoor Range & Outdoor Range
COST: Adults $10: 17 and under FREE: $40 year family membership.
Registration 9:00 to 11:00a.m, finish at 3:00pm
DIRECTIONS: See map at: www.greeleyarchers.com
DESCRIPTION: 40 3D targets at outdoor range.
CONTACT: Craig Weimer: 970-353-5368 after 6:30 P.M.
c.weimer@comcast.net

Greeley Archers Indoor Range
651 10th Avenue, Greeley CO

Greeley Archers Outdoor Range
42nd St & Belmont Ave
Evans CO 80620

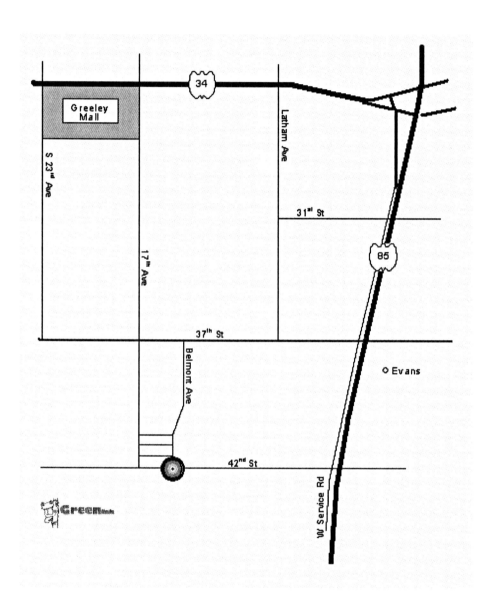

NAME: **Iron Rose Archery**
LOCATION: 16855 Bradshaw Rd. Peyton, CO 80831-9415
TYPE: Indoor Range- Private. Non-members welcome
COST: $ 10 per night
DIRECTIONS: From I25, Hwy 24 East 18 miles to Bradshaw Rd North 4.2 Miles
DESCRIPTION: 10 lanes up to 40 yards – Open Fri. 6-10 PM
CONTACT: Mike or Tracy Lee 719-749-2584 www.ironrosearchery.com

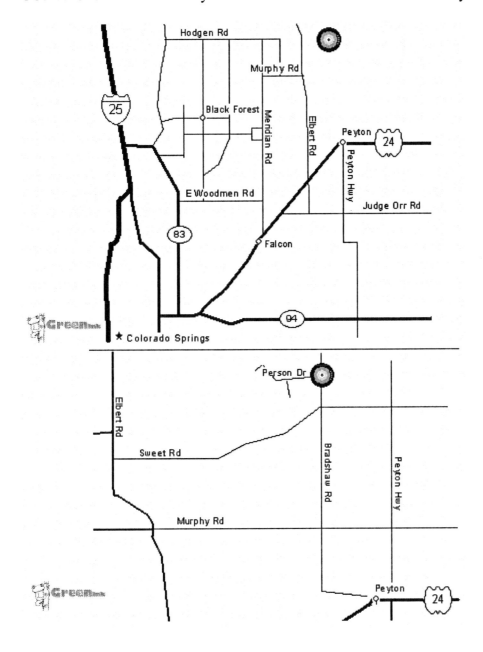

NAME: **Lon Hagler Reservoir**
LOCATION: Loveland, CO
TYPE: Outdoor Course
COST: Free to the public. Must have a Habitat Stamp.
DIRECTIONS: From I25 take Hwy. 14th St SE West approx. 7 miles. Turn Left on Cummings Ave. Take second right on W County Road 16e to end of road.
DESCRIPTION: Excelsior bales. Must have a Habitat Stamps can be obtained at WalMarts or anywhere hunting licenses are sold.
CONTACT: Lake 970-472-4460 or Big Thompson Bowhunters who maintain the Course. 970-663-4211 or 970-218-1047 or 303-776-5277

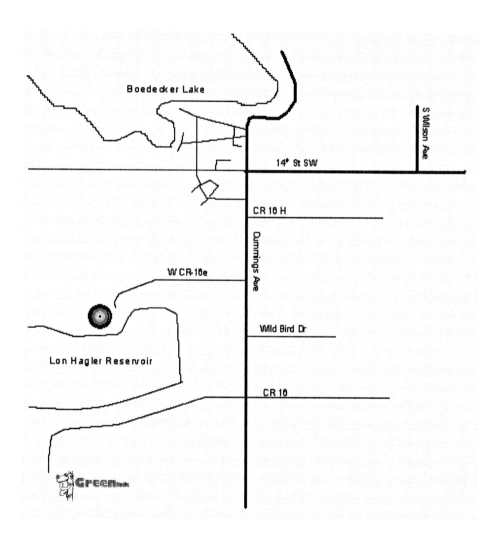

NAME: **May Farms**
LOCATION: 64001 East Highway 36 Byers, CO 80103
TYPE: 3D Courses
COST: Call for events
DIRECTIONS: Located minutes east of Denver on Colorado's high plains
DESCRIPTION: Don't miss out on a full weekend centered around the amazing sport of bow hunting! This fun filled weekend will showcase a variety of live music, hunter safety courses, exhibitor seminars, hayrides, barrel train rides, pony rides, bounce castle, animal barnyard, novelty target shoots, and farm amenities! Participate or just watch target shooters of all experience levels shoot along the Bijou Creek at May Farms. We'll have FORTY 3-D targets on the Bijou plus fly fishing demonstrations plus lessons and...
CONTACT: Gary May 303-822-5800 garym@mayfarms.com www.mayfarms.com

Illustration – May Farms

May Farms
64001 East Highway 36
Byers, CO
80103

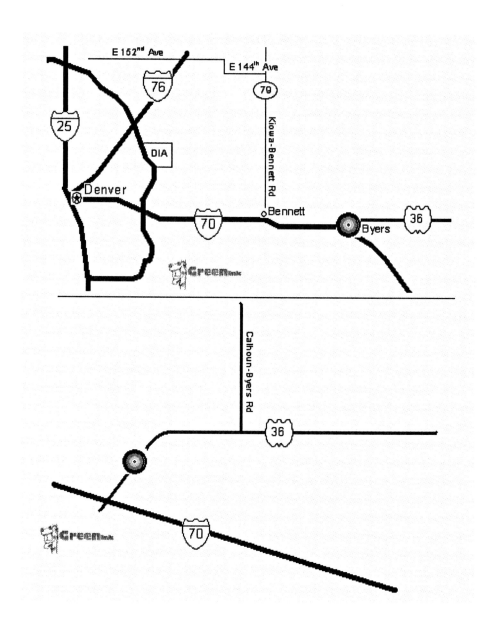

www.planetwildlife.net

NAME: **Mesa Verde Archers**
LOCATION: Cortez, CO
TYPE: Private Outdoor Course and Range
COST: $5.00 per person
DIRECTIONS: Contact *Outdoor Connections,* 101 N Broadway in Cortez. Telephone #970-565-6800 to pay entrance fee for gate combination and get directions to course.
DESCRIPTION: Good parking and toilet facilities. Beautiful Mesa Verde Country, 2 courses a short course and long course. Target opportunities are multi varied and well planed. At times one is working ones way through the arroyos trailing off the mesa then a quick passage up the cliff face and you are up on the mesa top strolling table flat lands engaging target opportunities among the pinion forests. Then another quick passage down the cliff face and one is back down in the valley engaging targets up on the cliff
CONTACT: Bill Kibel 970-565-6800

Illustration Mesa Verde 1

Illustration Mesa Verde 2

Mesa Verde Archers
Mesa Verde National Park,
Cortez CO 81328

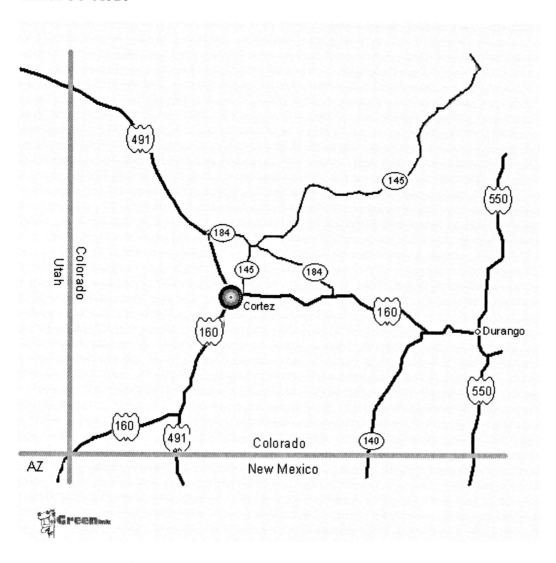

NAME: **Piedra Bowhunters**
LOCATION: PO Box 185, Monte Vista, CO 81144
TYPE: Outdoor Course
COST: Membership Dues are $25.00 per year which includes your immediate family (i.e. paid member, spouse, and any children under the age of 18) With a paid membership you are welcome to go as often as you like.
DIRECTIONS: Leave Monte Vista heading South 2 miles on HWY 15.
Turn right on Rock Creek Road (County Rd. 28) heading West and just keep driving making a hard left hand turn about 2.5 miles down the road. Stay on the pavement until it ends just after a bridge. There will be several little roads that lead to various other places but stay on the maintained road. When you get up the road a ways you will notice a log fence that is running on your left hand side. When this fence comes to an end you need to make a left. Our sign maybe hard to see (which is on the right hand side of the road) depending on how good the weather has been to us. If you have a GPS the left hand turn is at approximately @ (**Note all coordinates are in WGS 84 Format)
N37 28.282' W106 18.274'. When you make your hard left hand turn off of the maintained road into the "Archery Range" you will immediately cross a cattle guard. Just keep following the road from there and in just minutes you will see the sign up tables. Archery Range GPS coordinates are @ approximately N37 27.912' W106 18.259'
DESCRIPTION: The Piedra Bowhunters Archery Club, established in the early 1950's, is a family oriented club. We are a member of the Colorado Bowhunters Association. Our range is approximately 15 miles from Monte Vista, Colorado and located in the Rio Grande National Forest. We hold a 3D shoot on the second Sunday of June, July and August. There are 42 bales placed throughout the range.
CONTACT: (719) 655-2021 http://users.wildblue.net/piedra_bowhunter

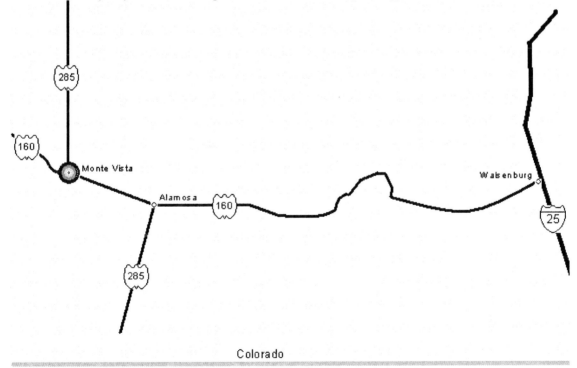

NAME: **Pikes Peak Gun Club**
LOCATION: 450 N Franceville Coalmine Rd. Colorado Springs, CO 80929
TYPE: Outdoor Range
COST: Annual membership. Single $122.00 first year, $97.50 renewal; Family $152.50 first year 127.50 renewal; Student $34.50 annual.
DIRECTIONS: From Colorado Springs go east on Highway 24(Platte Avenue) to the Highway 94 exit. Turn right on Highway 94 (east) and drive for 5.6 miles. Turn right on Franceville Coalmine Road for 1 mile. Turn right at the Pikes Peak Gun Club sign. Proceed to the clubhouse.
DESCRIPTION: Archery practice range at the gun club.
CONTACT: 719-683-4420 http://www.pikespeakgunclub.org

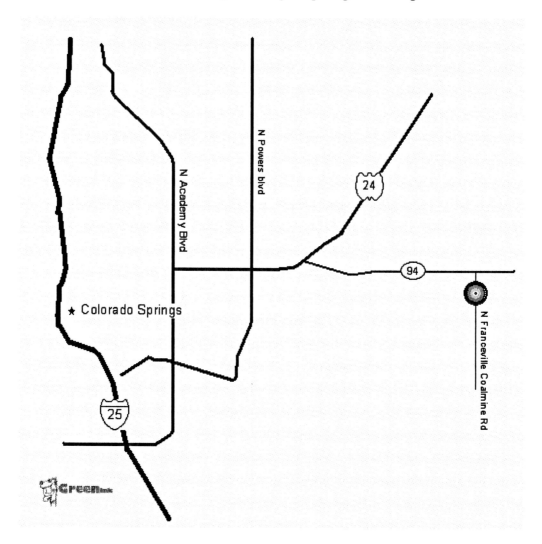

NAME: **Pueblo Mountain Park Archery Range**
LOCATION: Hwy 78 and Mountain Park Road, about 3 miles West of Beulah 81023.
TYPE: Outdoor Range - Public
COST: Free to the public
DIRECTIONS: About 3 miles West of Beulah on Hwy. 78
DESCRIPTION: Large targets placed at various yardages. Trails through forested area with targets offering shots of varying difficulty. Several shoots are offered during the year; contact representatives of the Pioneer Bowmen for more information.
CONTACT: 719-542-7739/4758

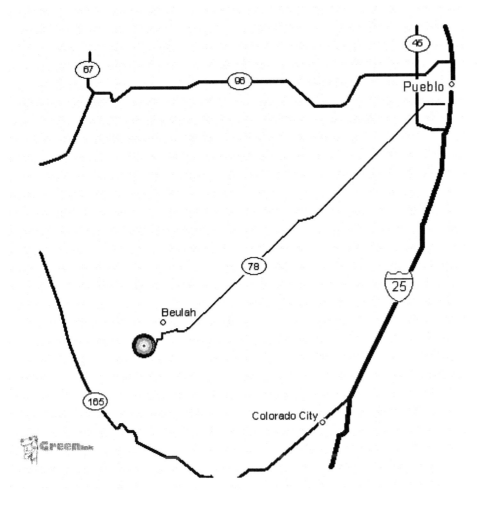

NAME: **Quail Run Sports**
LOCATION: 35027 County Road 27, Kiowa CO 80117
TYPE: Outdoor Range and Outdoor 3-D Course
COST: $12.00 per day
DIRECTIONS: From I25 take CO-86 East 17.0 miles. Turn Left on CR-27 for 0.7 miles.
DESCRIPTION: Outdoor Range is 10 lanes up to 60 yards at start of Course. Outdoor Course has 15 3-D targets in winter months and 40 targets during summer. There are 10 R/V spaces with power and water hookups and unlimited tent camping sights by the Range. Also ask about the Frontier Archery Club.
CONTACT: 303-646-3868

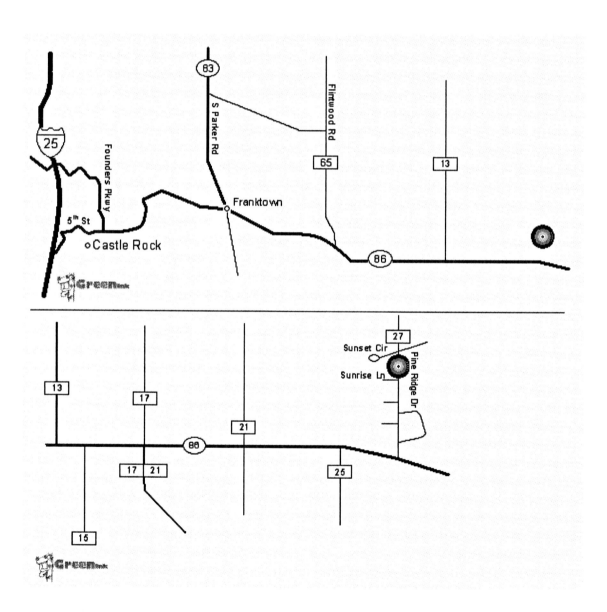

NAME: **Red Feather Bowmen**
LOCATION: PO Box 855, Paonia, CO 81428
TYPE: Indoor Range
COST: Free when accompanied by a member for first time visitors. Annual membership is $30.00 per family.
DIRECTIONS: Private club call for directions to Range.
DESCRIPTION: 8 lanes 20 yards
CONTACT: Diane Gallop 970-527-4152

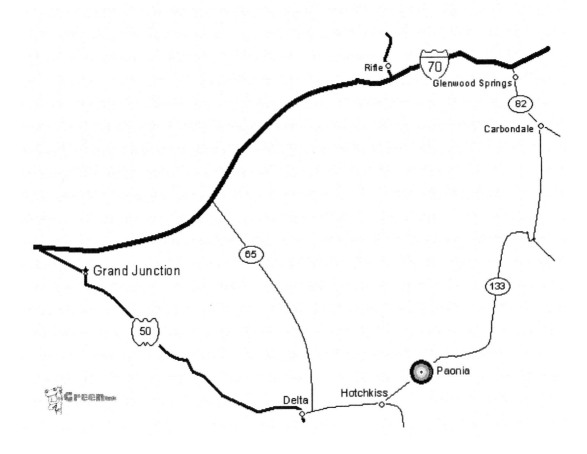

NAME: **Red Rock Archery**
LOCATION: 3193 Hall Ave. Grand Junction CO 81504
TYPE: Indoor Range & Video Hunting
COST: Range is $5.00 per day. Video is $10.00 per hour.
DIRECTIONS: From I70 take I-70 Business Loop West for 1.1 miles. Turn Left on 32nd Rd. for 0.3 miles. Turn Right to stay on 32nd Rd. for .01 miles. Turn Left on Hall Ave for 0.1 miles.
DESCRIPTION: Range is 22 lanes at 27 yards. Video hunting System has 5 lanes. Also ask about the Grand Mesa Bowmen Outdoor Course near Glade Park City.
CONTACT: 970-241-2697

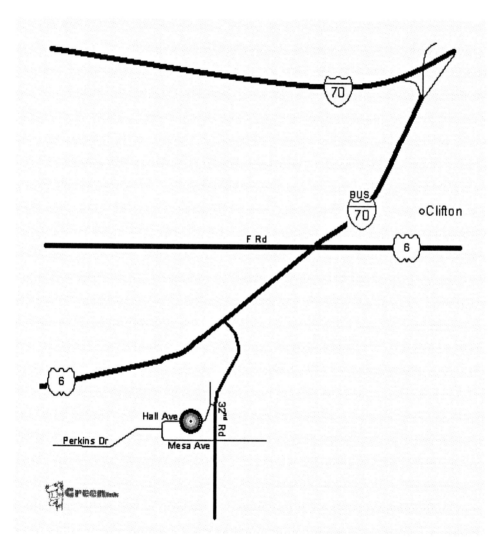

NAME: **Rocky Mountain Bowmen's Club**
LOCATION: Leadville CO
TYPE: Outdoor Range - Private
COST: Membership is $25.00 per year
DIRECTIONS: Approx. 20 miles South of I70 on Hwy. 24 to Airport entrance.
DESCRIPTION: Bow hunting club with 56 outdoor targets near Leadville
CONTACT: 719-486-3026

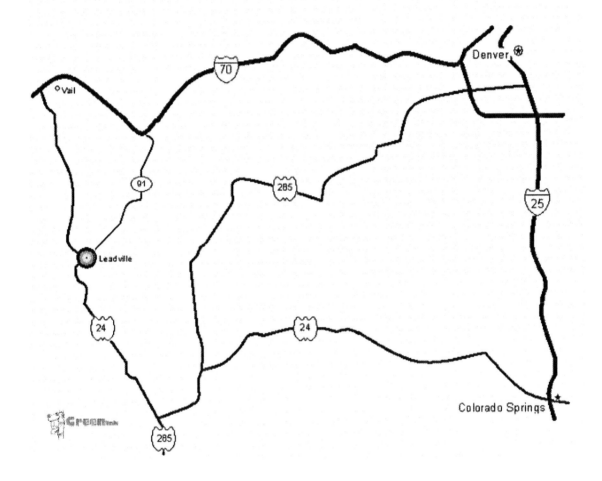

NAME: **Ski and Bow Rack**
LOCATION: 354 East Pagosa Street, Pagosa Springs, CO 81147
TYPE: Indoor Range; Techno Hunt
COST: Range $7.00, Techno Hunt $7.50 for a single shooter or $6.50 each for two shooters.
DIRECTIONS: Ski and Bow Rack is located on the east end of town off HWY 160.
DESCRIPTION: At Ski and Bow Rack, not only can you buy the equipment, you can put it to use on our seven-lane, 20 yard indoor range, featuring The Block backstops for easy arrow removal, or shoot Techno Hunt, computerized animal simulations for one of the most advanced and enjoyable ways to practice with your bow. Rental equipment and shooting lessons are also available.
CONTACT: 970-264-2370 www.skiandbowrack.com

Illustration Ski and Bow Rack Techno Hunt

Ski and Bow Rack
354 East Pagosa Street
Pagosa Springs, CO 81147

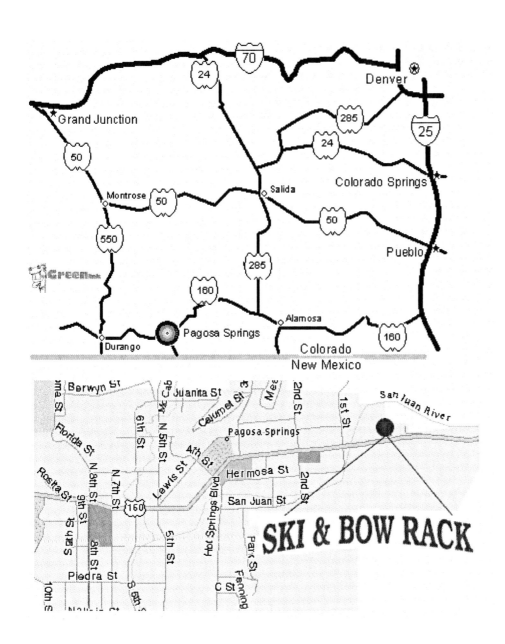

NAME:　　**Skyline Archery**
LOCATION:　Waterton, CO
TYPE:　　　Indoor Range
COST:　　　$15.00
DIRECTIONS:　Refer to map and call for directions.
DESCRIPTION:　Club Range, call ahead.
CONTACT:　James Gilmore 303-514-0254
james.q.gilmore.jr@lmco.com

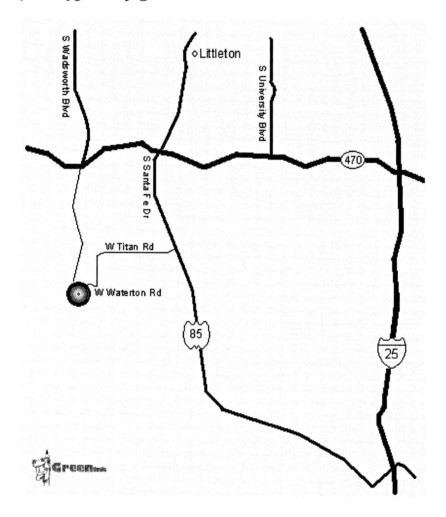

NAME: **St. Vrain Archery Club**
LOCATION: PO Box 92, Longmont, CO 80502
TYPE: Outdoor Course and Range
COST: Annual membership club. Initiation fee $40.00; single membership $25.00; couple $30.00; family $35.00. All members are expected to donate 8 hours of work time. Nonworking members pay an additional $50 non working fee.
DIRECTIONS: Saint Vrain Archery Range is located 4.6 miles East of Main Street on Hwy 119 (the new intersection of Pratt/119 and Main) and about 1.8 Miles West of I-25 on Hwy 119. This is Exit 240 off I-25. Look for the red topped building). Turn South on WCR 5. Go straight until you hit the first red gate (marked by the blue line). There is a second gate, also marked in blue, 350 yards from the first gate.
DESCRIPTION: Range open to members only. There is an east course of 14 targets and a west course of 14 targets the practice area is actually between the east and west course.
CONTACT: 303-651-6700 http://www.svarchery.org

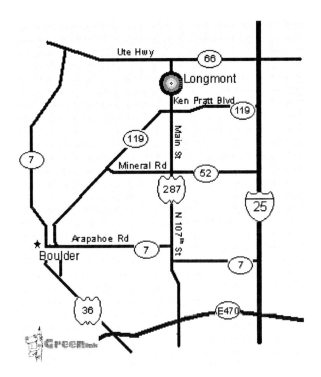

NAME: **Tanglewood Archery**
LOCATION: 7158 N Washington St. Denver, CO 80229
TYPE: Indoor Range, DART system
COST: Indoor Range $7.00/day; DART system $7.00/ ½ hour, $10.00/hour
DIRECTIONS: Downtown Denver location; refer to map.
DESCRIPTION: Indoor Range 20 lanes 20 yards, and DART system Tanglewood Archery also has a Dart System for the archer who wants some practice on moving targets. The Dart System consists of a video screen which displays real-life animals in the wild. Arrows are fitted with special tips and the shots are scored for and tracked. Practice your hunting shots or for even more fun, bring your buddies and compete for the best scores. Try shooting Moose, Whitetail Deer, Rocky Mountain Elk, Turkey or even Bears, and the list goes on, and on. There is even a Kid's Disc with fun moving cartoon targets! Also Ask about Golden High Country Archers Club who have a 28 3-D target Course near the Coors brewery.
CONTACT: 303-288-2126 (Tues-Fri 11-5)
http://www.tanglewoodarchery.com/Default.aspx

Illustration- Tanglewood archery Indoor Range

Tanglewood Archery
Denver, CO

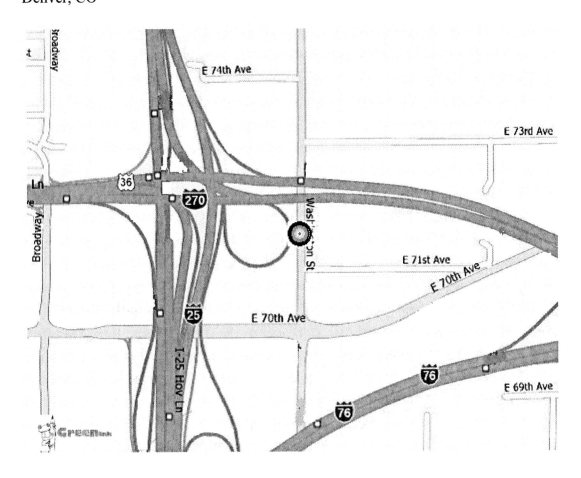

NAME: **White River Bowmen**
LOCATION: PO Box 32 Rangely, CO 81648
TYPE: Indoor Range
COST: Membership $50.00 family
DIRECTIONS: Call club for directions to Range
DESCRIPTION: 10 lanes, 20 yards
CONTACT: Glen Filener (evenings) 970-675-5727

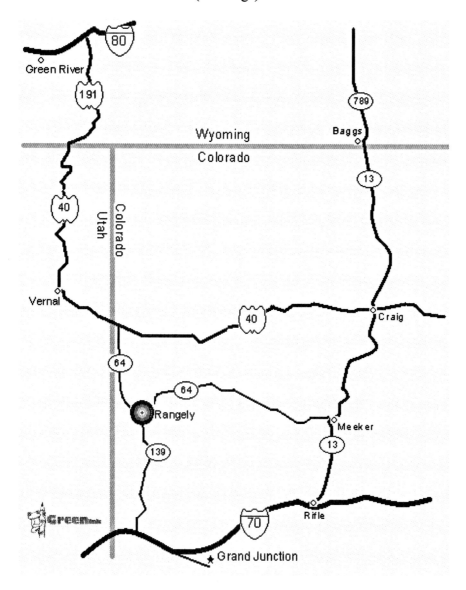

IDAHO Locations

- ☐ Archery Idaho
- ☐ Bitterroot Mountains Archers
- ☐ B J's 19th Hole Sports Tavern
- ☐ Blackfoot River Bowmen
- ☐ Blackfoot River Bowmen
- ☐ Bryan's Archery LLC
- ☐ Camas Prairie Bowmen
- ☐ Center Target Sports, Inc.
- ☐ Ee-Da-How
- ☐ Idaho Outdoor Outfitters
- ☐ Indianhead Bow hunters
- ☐ Lewis Clark Wildlife Club
- ☐ Magic Valley Bowhunters Club
- ☐ Minidoka Bowmen Club
- ☐ Mountain Home AFB Trap and Skeet Range
- ☐ Nampa Bow Chiefs
- ☐ Pocatello Field Archers
- ☐ Rocky Mountain Archery
- ☐ Rose Park
- ☐ Selkirk Archers
- ☐ Sure Shot Sporting Goods
- ☐ Up North Archers

NAME: **Archery Idaho**
LOCATION: 1363 Northgate Mile, Idaho Falls ID 83401-2012
TYPE: Indoor range in store
COST: $4.00 per hour
DIRECTIONS: From I15 take W Broadway St. East 0.8 miles. Turn Left on N Yellowstone Hwy (US-26) 1.4 miles.
DESCRIPTION: 10 lanes – 20 yards
CONTACT: 208- 524-0161
archeryidaho@cableone.net

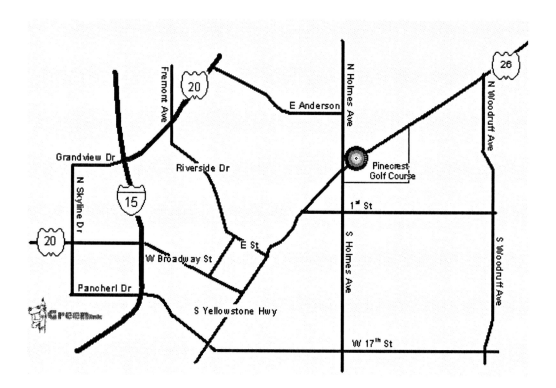

NAME: **Bitterroot Mountains Archers**
LOCATION: Osburn, ID 83849
TYPE: Indoor Range
COST: Free to visitors. Annual membership is $10 for individual; $25 for a Family.
DIRECTIONS: Cataldo Mission Exit and follow signs to shoot site
DESCRIPTION: Range is 12 lanes at 30 yards.
CONTACT: Ray Serrano 208-556-7802 aztecprohunter@yahoo.com

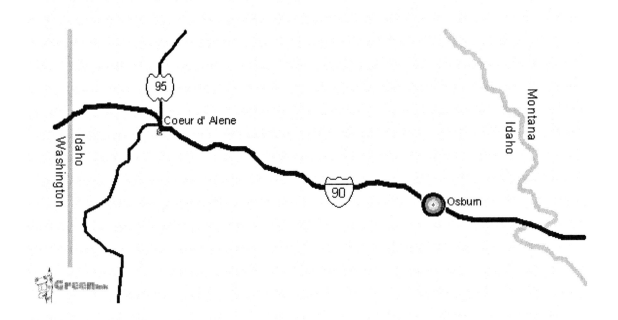

NAME: **B J's 19th Hole Sports Tavern**
LOCATION: 523 E 5th North, Burley ID 83318-3463
TYPE: Indoor 3-D video
COST: $6.00 per hour and $3.00 ea. for special arrow tips (or you can just borrow the tips for Free).
DIRECTIONS: From I84 turn South on ID-27 for 1.5 miles. Turn Left on E 5th St for 0.3 miles.
DESCRIPTION: 3-D video screen in a cozy local setting. Almost like the real thing.
CONTACT: 208-679-9070

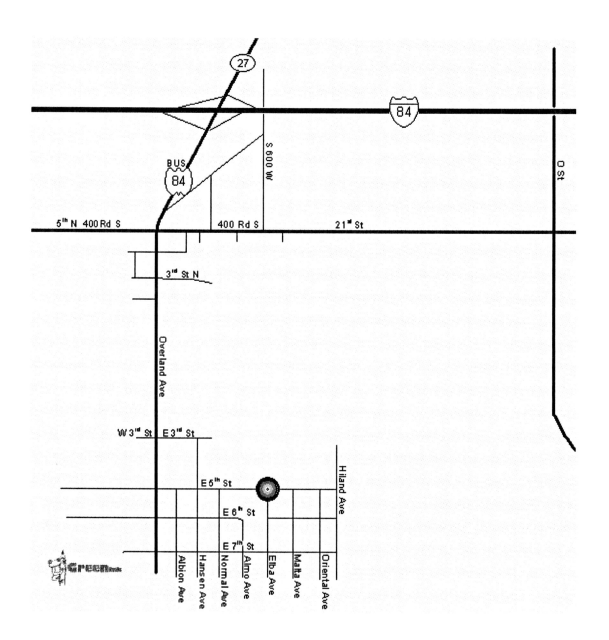

NAME: **Blackfoot River Bowmen**
LOCATION: Blackfoot, ID
TYPE: Outdoor Course and Range, Indoor Range
COST: $2.00 visitors
DIRECTIONS: The Blackfoot River Bowmen range is located in the Rose Pond recreational area just north of Blackfoot, Idaho.
DESCRIPTION The archery range sits on ground leased from Bingham County and includes three outdoor ranges. Each of the ranges consists of 20 cardboard butts and burlap targets. The terrain is very mild and easily navigable by almost everyone. Currently we have two elevated shooting platforms giving shooters the opportunity to gain the perspective of being in a tree stand. We hold a variety of 3-D shoots during the year and they typically have as many as 40 life-size animal targets.
CONTACT: Rob Allen 208-223-3534 john@1jo.myrf.net www.brbarchery.com

Blackfoot River Bowmen
Blackfoot ID

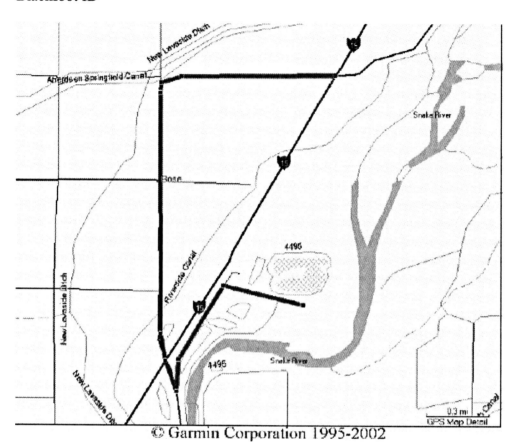

© Garmin Corporation 1995-2002

www.planetwildlife.net

NAME: **Bryan's Archery LLC**
LOCATION: 1851 Main St. Lewiston ID
TYPE: Indoor range
COST: $6.00 per hour
DIRECTIONS: Refer to map and/or call for directions.
DESCRIPTION: Range is 10 lanes – 20 yards
CONTACT: 208-746-7977

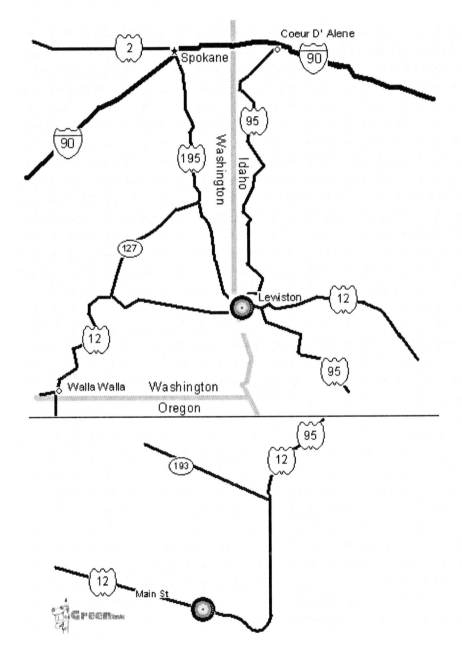

NAME: **Camas Prairie Bowmen**
LOCATION: Grangeville, ID
TYPE: Outdoor Range
COST: For members. Annual membership is $20.00 per individual.
DIRECTIONS: Approx. 3 miles South of Grangeville on Salmon Rd.
DESCRIPTION: 28 bail targets.
CONTACT: Harold 208-983-0287 bryansarchery1@clearwire.net

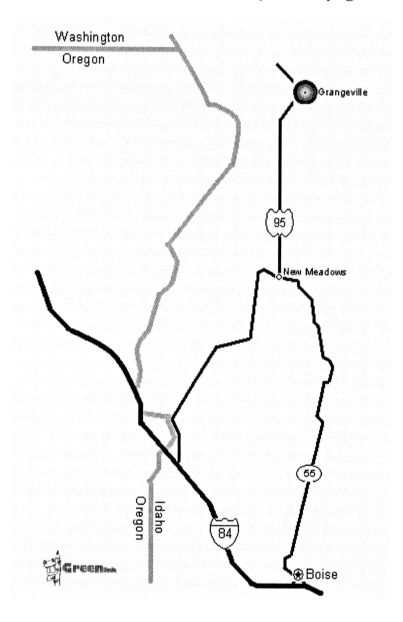

NAME: **Center Target Sports, Inc.**
LOCATION: 3295 E Mullan Ave. Post Falls, ID 83854
TYPE: Indoor Range
COST: $10.00 all day
DIRECTIONS: From I90 take exit 7 turn north on highway 41, turn west on E Mullan Ave. This is a fire arms range that caters to Archery on Friday and Saturday nights at 6:00 pm.
DESCRIPTION: 15 Indoor Lanes each 25 yards long with automatic target retrieval
CONTACT: 208-773-2331 www.centertargetsports.com

Illustration - Center target Sports

Center Target Sports, Inc.
3295 E Mullan Ave. Post Falls, ID 83854

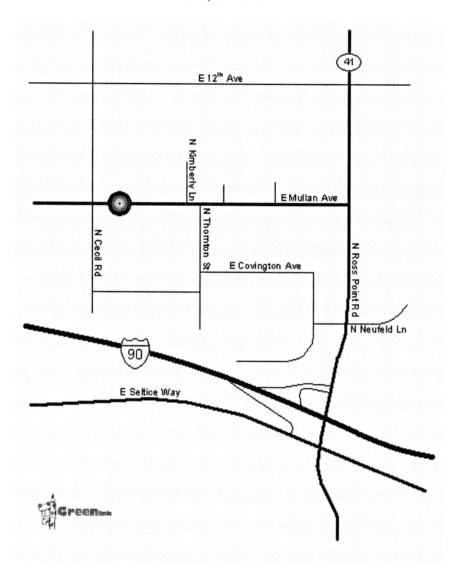

www.planetwildlife.net

NAME: **Ee-Da-How**
LOCATION: Moscow, ID
TYPE: Indoor Range & Outdoor Course
COST: For members only. Annual membership is $30.00 per individual and $40.00 per family.
DIRECTIONS: Refer to map and call ahead for directions.
DESCRIPTION: 28 target course just North of Moscow. Indoor Range is open Mondays only.
CONTACT: Dick 208-743-6473 dakotadick@hotmail.com

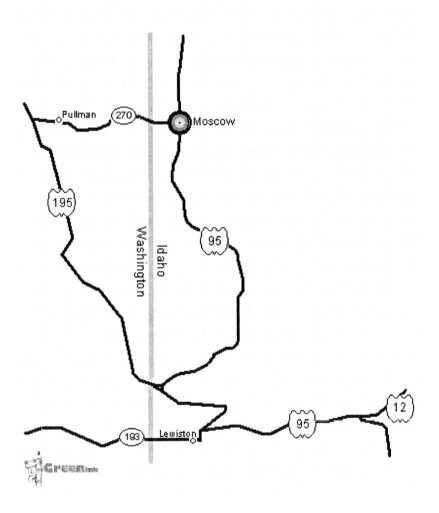

NAME: **Idaho Outdoor Outfitters**
LOCATION: 3226 Garrity Blvd Nampa, ID 83687
TYPE: Indoor Techno Hunt, Outdoor 3D Course
COST: Techno Hunt- single shooter $15/ ½ hour; 2 or more shooters $30/ hour.
Course $10/ hour; 15 visits pass $100.00
DIRECTIONS: From I-84 take exit 38; go southwest on Garrity Blvd. Store is just befor Airport Rd.
DESCRIPTION: Techno hunt accommodates up to 4 shooters. Outdoor course 15 - 3D Targets with 3 moving targets and 2 fall-away targets.
CONTACT: 208-467-5961

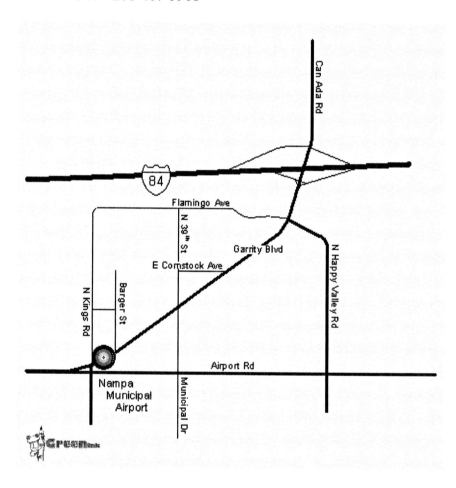

NAME: **Indianhead Bow hunters**
LOCATION: Weiser, ID
TYPE: Indoor Range
COST: Range Key Pass rates are:
$120.00/Year Single (Adult or Youth, Includes IHB Membership)
$200.00/Year Family (Two Adult shooters and kids under 18 living at home, Includes IHB Membership)
Non-Pass holders pay $5/Day Adult & Youth, and $2.50/day Kids rates
DIRECTIONS: Refer to map and call for directions.
DESCRIPTION: Range Key Privileges (March to March) include, IHB membership, winter league shooting, and any open day shooting as well as anytime you want to shoot that the range is not being used by other groups, classes, or sponsors. Please do not abuse the key pass, and help welcome all sponsors and visiting shooters.
CONTACT: Craig Doan 208-549-1063 cdnbd@ruralnetwork.net
www.idahoarchery.com/ihb

Illustration - Indianhead Bow hunters Indoor Range

Indianhead Bow hunters
Weiser, ID

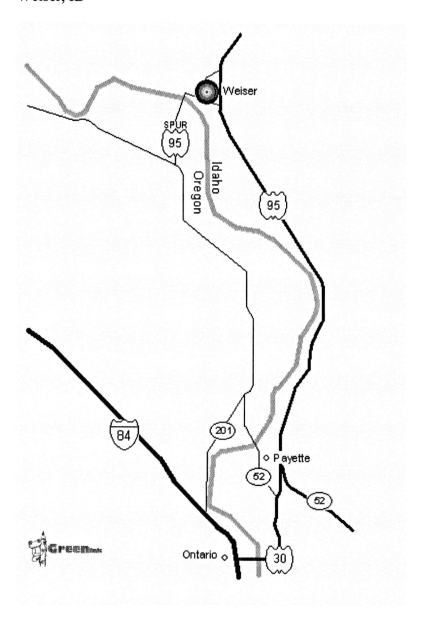

www.planetwildlife.net

NAME: **Lewis Clark Wildlife Club**
LOCATION: PO Box 146 Lewiston, ID 83501
TYPE: Indoor and Outdoor Range
COST: The range fees: $3.00 for members $8.00 for non-members
DIRECTIONS: The Lewis-Clark Wildlife Range is located 25 miles SE of Lewiston on the South Tom Beall Road. From Lewiston just head south toward Lapwai on Highway 95. Go east on the Tom Beall turn off about a mile before you get to Lapwai. When you get to the Y take the right fork, South Tom Beall Road. 4.5 miles down the road and you will find the range on the left.
DESCRIPTION: Indoor Range and Outdoor shooting Range in a protected Valley. Also gun Range distances up to 200 yards.
CONTACT: 208-843-2987 www.lcwildlife.org

Illustration- Lewis Clark Wildlife Range

Lewis Clark Wildlife Club

Lewiston, ID 83501

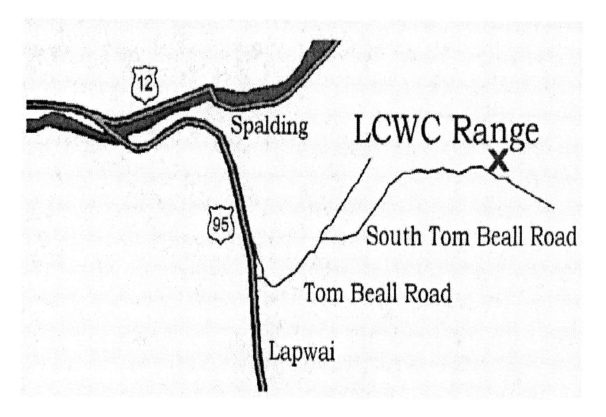

NAME: **Magic Valley Bowhunters Club**
LOCATION: PO Box 1105, Twin Falls, ID 83303
TYPE: Indoor Range and outdoor Range
COST: Annual Membership. Single membership $30 (with key $50); Family Membership $50 (with key $70)
DIRECTIONS: Located on corner of 2nd Ave S and Shashone downstairs below ballroom.
DESCRIPTION: The Magic Valley Bowhunters Club has been dedicated to promoting and protecting the great sport of archery and bowhunting for nearly 50 years. OT-YO-KWA, (meaning Brotherhood in the Algonquin language), is the foundation from which we build our membership. The Magic Valley Bowhunters understand that the future of archery and bowhunting lies in the hands of our youth. We offer special programs and leagues for all age groups, genders and levels of ability all the while promoting wildlife conservation, land stewardship and the ethical conduct that archers and bow hunters are required to practice at all times.
CONTACT: 208-733-3689 http://www.idahoarchery.com/mvb/default.asp

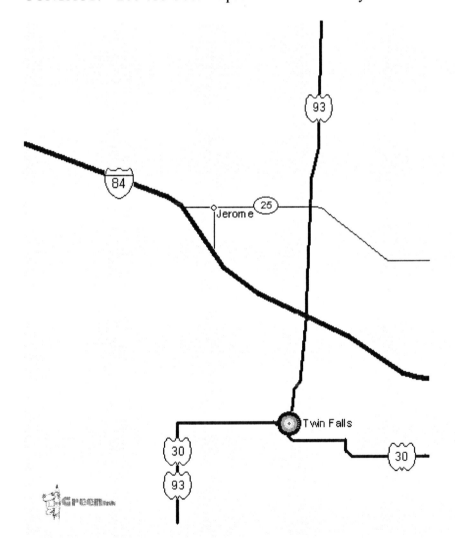

NAME: **Minidoka Bowmen Club**
LOCATION: Rupert, ID
TYPE: Indoor Range & Outdoor Course
COST: $3.00 per night. Annual membership is $25.00 for an individual and $35.00 for a family.
DIRECTIONS: Approx 3.5 miles North of I84 on Hwy 24.
DESCRIPTION: Indoor Range is 8 lanes at 20 yards. Outdoor Course is 14 targets ranging from 20 to 50 yards by the local dam.
CONTACT: Matt Fetzer 208-219-0736 bbynrse@pmt.org

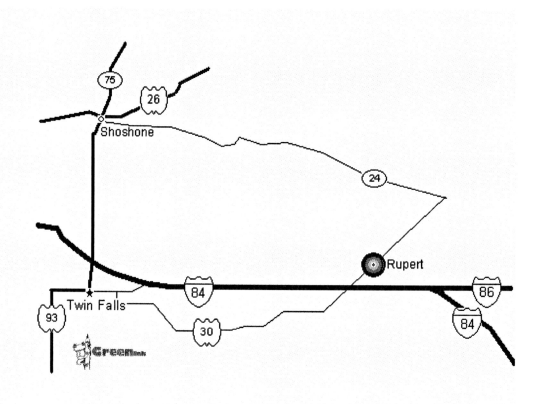

NAME: **Mountain Home AFB Trap and Skeet Range**
LOCATION: 366 Svs/Svrt 710 Trap Dr, Mountain Home AFB, ID 83648
TYPE: Outdoor Range (on Base)
COST: $3.00/ day; seasonal passes available call for price
DIRECTIONS: Must be able to access base
DESCRIPTION: 8 lanes 20,40,60,80 yards targets
CONTACT: 208-828-6288

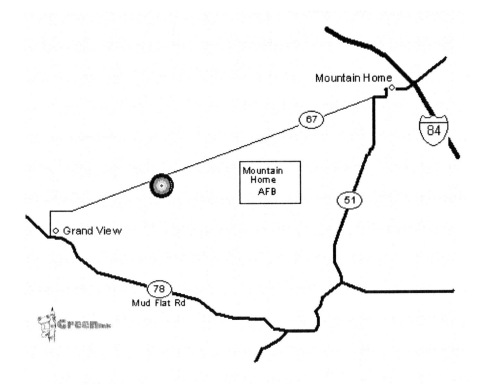

NAME: **Nampa Bow Chiefs**
LOCATION: 222 W Railroad St. Nampa, ID 83687-8208
TYPE: Private, Indoor range
COST: Annual membership - $100 individual - $140 family
DIRECTIONS: From I84 take Nampa Blvd. South 0.6 miles. Take a Sharp Right on Northside Blvd. for 0.1 miles. Turn Left on W Railroad St. for 0.1 miles.
DESCRIPTION: The Nampa Bow Chiefs is a well rounded archery organization, supporting bow hunting and target shooting for all ages. We have an indoor shooting range where we host fall and winter leagues of various formats, allowing archers to hone and maintain their shooting skills when the weather isn't conducive to outdoor shooting. There is also an outdoor range at the Nampa Bow Chiefs facility with permanent target fixtures, ranging from 20 to 50 yards that is open to the public.
CONTACT: Russ 208-466-4374
http://www.idahoarchery.com/nbc/

Nampa Bow Cheifs
222 W Railroad St, Nampa,ID 83651

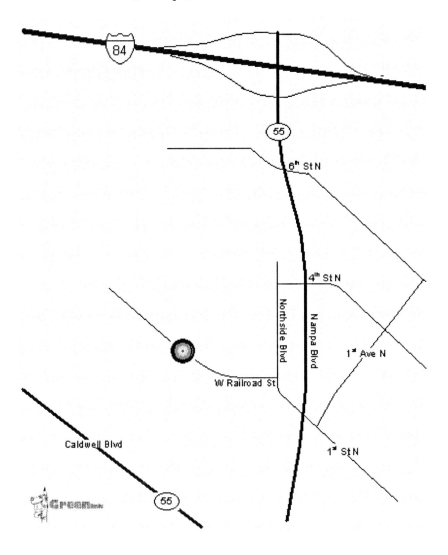

NAME: **Pocatello Field Archers**
LOCATION: Pocatello, ID
TYPE: 1 Indoor & 2 Outdoor Ranges
COST: Family (Parents and children under 18)=$65.00 Single = $50.00 Senior 60+ $20.00 Junior/College = $27.50 Lifetime Family (2 Members only) $750.00 Lifetime Single = $500.00
DIRECTIONS: Approx. two miles south of the I15 and I86 junction.
DESCRIPTION: 1 Indoor range with 16 lanes, Restrooms, bleachers, kitchen, and meeting room. Belong to a membership club, with a low membership beginning August 1 and ending on July 31 of the next year. Members use key to unlock gates and doors at all ranges but can use the Pocatello Cr Ranges on a 24/7 basis, unless there is a previous commitment. JOAD/youth classes are given twice a year (8 Weeks) by 2 certified teachers. Youth Groups, Scouts, Schools, and the college hold classes with-in the range. Also includes 2 outdoor ranges, Pocatello Creek & Scout Mt.
CONTACT: Beebe 208-233-5196 beebebow@yahoo.com

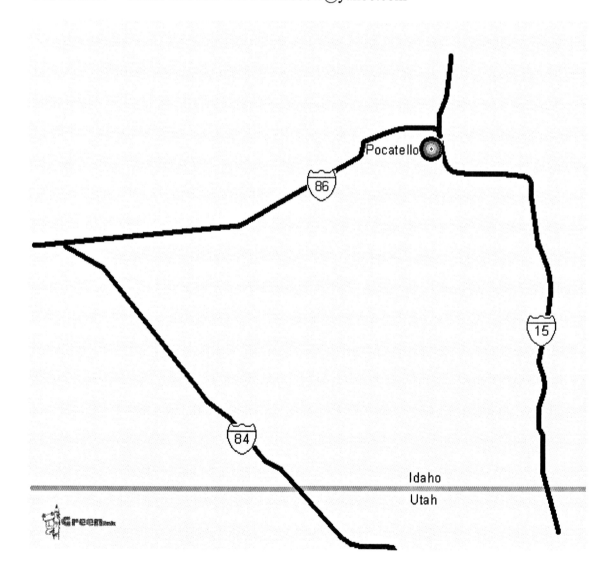

NAME: **Rocky Mountain Archery**
LOCATION: 29794 N Wheatridge Rd. Athol, ID 83801
TYPE: Indoor range
COST: $3.00 per hour
DIRECTIONS: From I-90 take N Lincoln Way (US-95) north approx 18 miles. Turn Left on ID-54 1.3 miles. Turn Left on N Wheatridge Rd. 0.3 miles.
DESCRIPTION: Range is 6 lanes – 20 yards. Open after 12:00 noon.
CONTACT: 208-683-3676

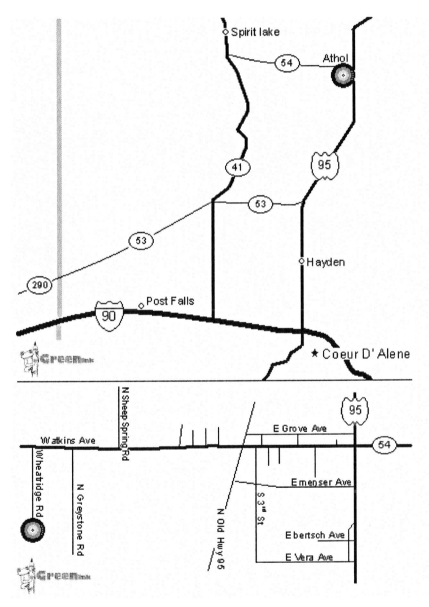

NAME: **Rose Park**
LOCATION: 501 N Maple St. #206, Blackfoot ID 83221-1700
TYPE: Indoor and Outdoor range
COST: Park fee allows access.
DIRECTIONS: From I15 take 15 business rout East. Turn Left on SW Main St. Turn left on W Washington St. and proceed to end of street.
DESCRIPTION: This recreation area features a 40-acre fishing lake and a fine indoor and outdoor archery ranges. The County Archery Range at Rock Park is home to the Blackfoot River Bowmen Club.
CONTACT: 208-782-3190 The Bingham County Parks & Recreation Office hours are Monday-Friday 8:00 a.m.-5:00 p.m.

Illustration - Rose Park Range

Rose Park

501 N Maple St. #206, Blackfoot ID 83221-1700

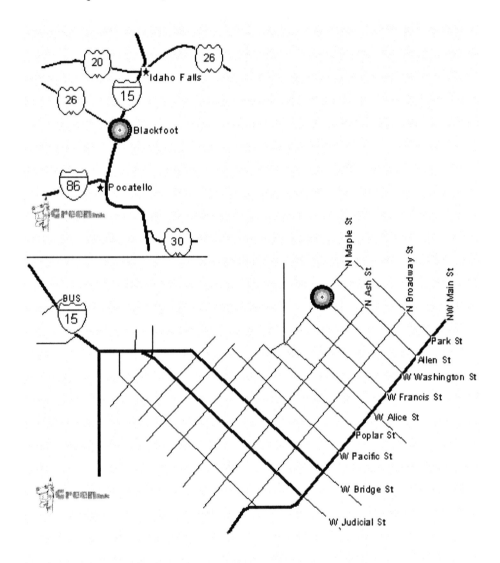

NAME: **Selkirk Archers**
LOCATION: Bonners Ferry, ID
TYPE: Indoor Range, Outdoor Course (summers)
COST: Annual membership, individual $20.00 Call for family discounts.
DIRECTIONS: Private club, Call for Directions
DESCRIPTION: Indoor range 10 lanes 20 yards. Outdoor course constantly evolving 15-18 targets in different configurations.
CONTACT: 208-267-7223

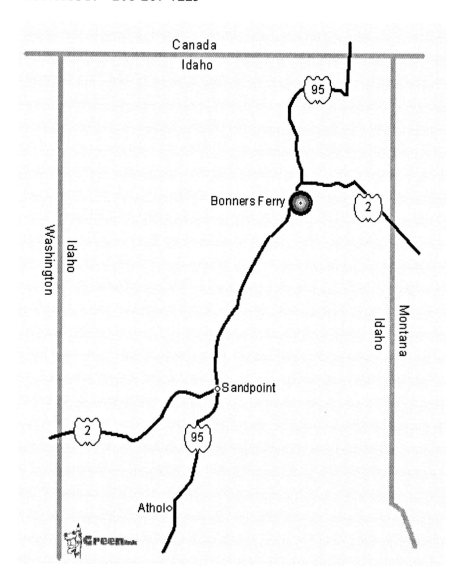

NAME: **Sure Shot Sporting Goods**
LOCATION: 1016 W Pullman Rd. Moscow ID 83843
TYPE: Indoor Range
COST: Free to customers
DIRECTIONS: From US-95 take hwy 8 West Approx 0.6 miles.
DESCRIPTION: Indoor Range has 2 Lanes / 10 Yards
CONTACT: 208-882-1483

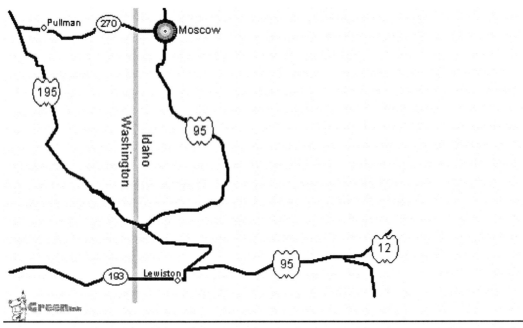

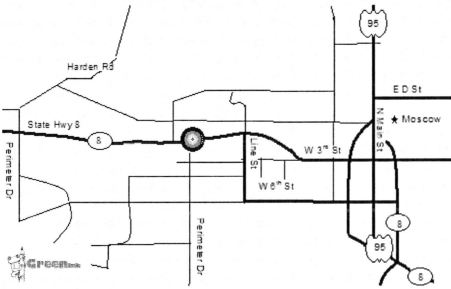

NAME: **Up North Archers**
LOCATION: 3391 East Side Road, Priest River, ID 83856
TYPE: Indoor range in store
COST: $5.00 per hour
DIRECTIONS: From I90 take Ross Point-Rathdrum Hwy (ID-41) North 38.6 miles. Turn Right on Walnut St (US-2) 5.8 miles. Turn Left on 9th St. (N ID-57) 3.5 miles. Turn Right on Peninsula Rd. 4.3 miles. Turn Left on McCabe Falls Rd. 4.0 miles. McCabe Falls Rd becomes Eastside Rd (portions unpaved) 1.7 miles.
DESCRIPTION: Up to 40 yards and up to 60 yards in summer
CONTACT: John Scribner 208-448-1837 lucky@icce.com

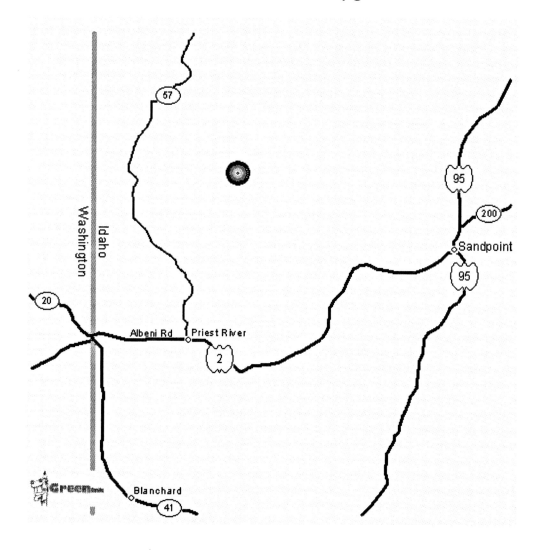

MONTANA Locations

- ☐ 3D Archery Supply
- ☐ Archer's Den & Taxidermy
- ☐ Bear Paw Bowmen
- ☐ Big Sky Archery
- ☐ Billings Rod and Gun Club
- ☐ Buffalo Jump Archery
- ☐ Capital Sports & Western
- ☐ Don Archery
- ☐ Electric City Archers
- ☐ The Elusive Moose
- ☐ Five Valleys Archery Club
- ☐ Great Falls Archery Club
- ☐ Judith Basin Archery Club
- ☐ Lewis and Clark Archers
- ☐ Libby Archery Club
- ☐ Lone Pine State Park
- ☐ Marias Valley Archers
- ☐ Milk River Archery
- ☐ Rocky Mountain Archery
- ☐ Spirit Quest Archery
- ☐ Superior Archery, Inc.
- ☐ Uncle Bob's Outdoors
- ☐ Windy River Archery Club
- ☐ Yellowstone Bowmen
- ☐ Yellowstone Gateway Sports
- ☐ Young Life Bowfest

NAME: **3D Archery Supply**
LOCATION: 775 Coach Ave. Vaughn, MT 59487
TYPE: Indoor range
COST: $3.00/ Day
DIRECTIONS: From I-15 take Exit 290 head west on 89/200, turn north on 4th street, turn west on Couch Ave.
DESCRIPTION: 8 Lanes up to 40 yards
CONTACT: 406-965-3236

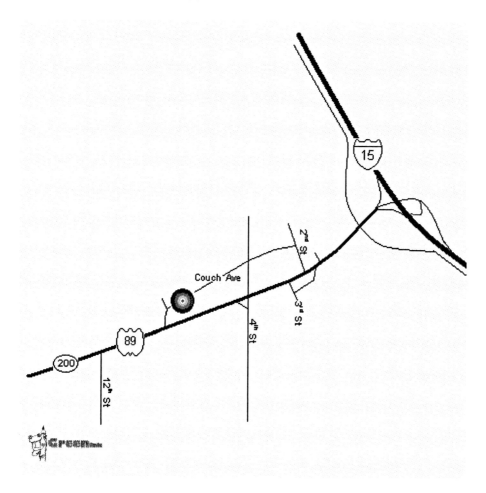

NAME: **Archer's Den & Taxidermy**
LOCATION: 1318 River Drive N, Great Falls MT 59401-1325
TYPE: Indoor Range
COST: $5.00 per day; $30.00 per month or $75.00 per quarter
DIRECTIONS: From I-15 take Central Ave. W East Bount to River Dr. N North bound.
DESCRIPTION: Range is 10 lanes at 20 yards
CONTACT: 406-452-1921

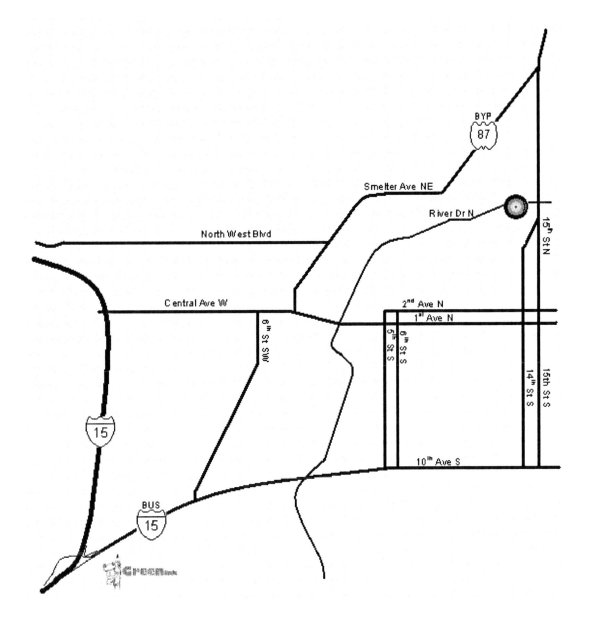

NAME: **Bear Paw Bowmen**
LOCATION: Havre MT
TYPE: Indoor Range
COST: Call
DIRECTIONS: From I15 at Great Falls take US-87 approx. 109 miles North.
DESCRIPTION: Private Hunting Club has 20 yard range at local shopping center.
Currently members only who have just acquired range. May rent for daily use soon.
Call.
CONTACT: Nick Siebrasse 406-395-4844 www.bearpawbowmen.com

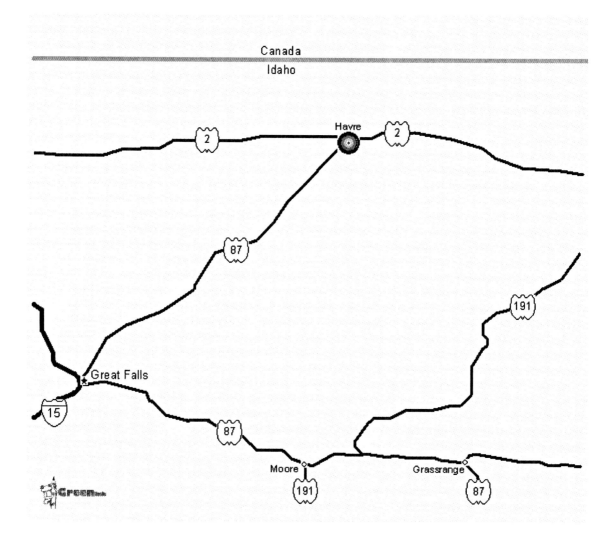

NAME: **Big Sky Archery**
LOCATION: 120 Pollywog Lane, Belgrade, Mt 59714
TYPE: Indoor Range; 3D and Techno Hunt
COST: Fees for ranges: Day - $6; 10 Day Passes - $50; Year Pass - $125
Fees for the Techno Hunt: 1 shooter: $10 ½ hour, $18 hour;
2 shooters $9 ½ hour, $17 hour; 3+shooters $8 ½ hour, $15 hour.
DIRECTIONS: Refer to map and call ahead for directions
DESCRIPTION: Come in and spend an unlimited day pass in our 20, 25, or 35 yard ranges. We have bulls-eye, animal paper targets, and 3D animal targets including deer, antelope, and small animals. Shoot your arrow through our chronograph and see just how fast it can fly! Paper and 3D targets are great for fine-tuning the accuracy and precision of you and your equipment, but what about actually testing that on moving targets? Our Techno Hunt video target system allows you to shoot a variety of game and small animals in real-life situations. You can shoot the system "as-is" at 20 yards, or we can program it to give you a real challenge with actual yardages and wind speeds that you have to account for when you aim.
CONTACT: 406-388-0503 www.bigskyarchery.com

Illustration indoor 3D targets

Big Sky Archery
120 Pollywog Lane,
Belgrade, Mt
59714

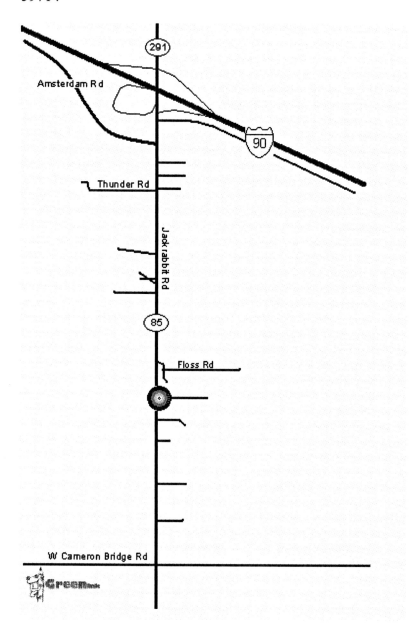

NAME: **Billings Rod and Gun Club**

LOCATION: PO Box 33, Billings, Mt 59103

TYPE: Outdoor Range and Course

COST: Annual membership dues $85. Collegiate memberships $20/year.

DIRECTIONS: Billings Rod and Gun Club is located west of Logan International Airport on Rod and Gun Club Road.

DESCRIPTION: Archers can choose from 6 different ranges to hone their skills. One sight-in range is located in front of the main clubhouse, the second is just South of the Sporting Clays building and range. Both feature target butts placed every 5 yards out to 80 yards. A sand filled bunker is provided west of the sight-in range for those wishing to shoot broad head tipped arrows. Brodhead tips are allowed only at the sight-in range bunker. Two of the four archery trails start behind the main clubhouse. The other two start at the NW corner of the parking lot near the Shotgun Division clubhouse.

CONTACT: 406-259-0006 www.billingsrodandgun.org

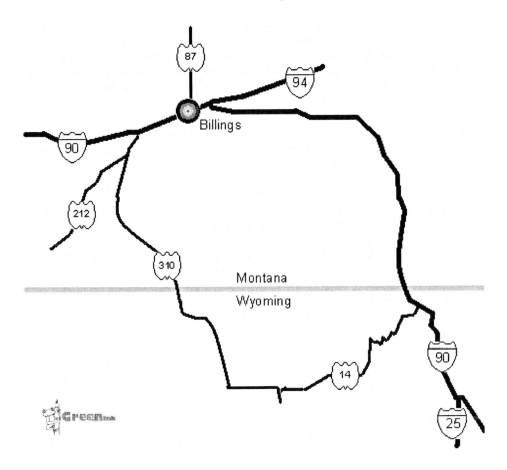

NAME: **Buffalo Jump Archery**
LOCATION: 2710 Broadwater Ave. Helena MT 59602
TYPE: Indoor and outdoor ranges
COST: $5.00 per hour for outdoor Range. $7.00 per hour for 3-D.
DIRECTIONS: We offer two locations to better serve our clients: 25 minutes west of Bozeman near Three Forks, and in Helena in the old Kessler Brewing facility on the west side just off highway 12.
DESCRIPTION: Our facilities host a full line of equipment and accessories, expert technicians and package deals you won't find anywhere else. We also offer in our Three Forks store two 20 target outdoor 3D ranges spring to fall and a 30 target 3D indoor range in winter. Open Wednesdays through Sundays. Professional instructors available.
CONTACT: Judy or Jarod Adams (406) 285-4111 adamsjg2000@yahoo.com
www.buffalojumparchery.com

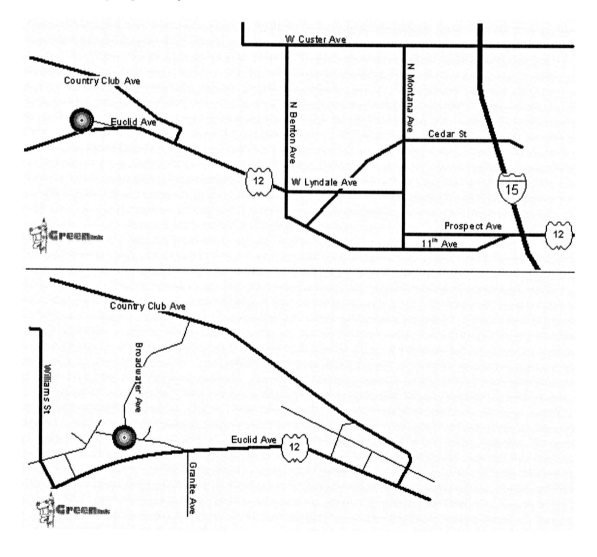

NAME: **Capital Sports & Western**
LOCATION: 1092 Helena Ave. Helena MT 59601-3573
TYPE: Indoor Range
COST: Free for customers
DIRECTIONS: From I-15 take Prospect Ave. West. Turn Right on N Dakots St. Turn Left on Helena Ave.
DESCRIPTION: Range is 1 lane and 10 to 20 yards.
CONTACT: 406-443-2978

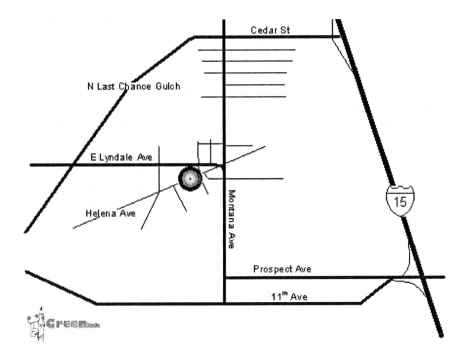

NAME: **Don Archery**
LOCATION: 120 Second Ave South, Lewistown, MT 59457-3026
TYPE: Indoor range and Outdoor Range
COST: Indoor free, Outdoor $30.00 per year
DIRECTIONS: From Billings on I-90, take US-87 North approx. 120 miles. Turn Left on 2nd Ave. S 0.1 miles.
DESCRIPTION: 1 lane/30 yards
CONTACT: Contact Dons for permit at 800-879-8194 Web: montanaarchery.com

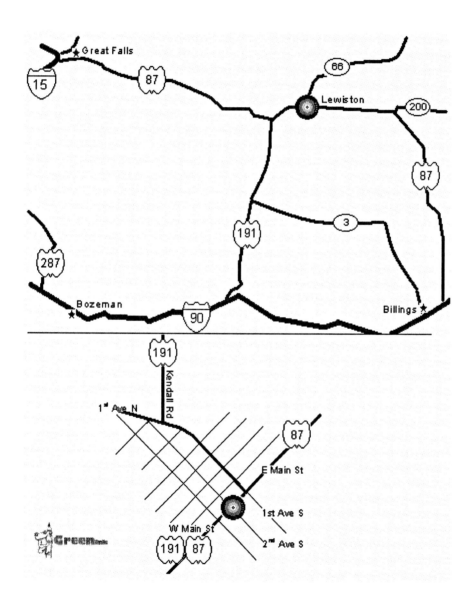

NAME: **Electric City Archers**
LOCATION: Wadsworth Park, Great Falls MT
TYPE: Local Club/Outdoor Archery Range
COST: $40 single, $50Family
DIRECTIONS: Wadsworth Park located 2 miles west of city limits
DESCRIPTION: Outdoor Range
CONTACT: Joel McNeese 406-727-2997 mcneese@mcn.net

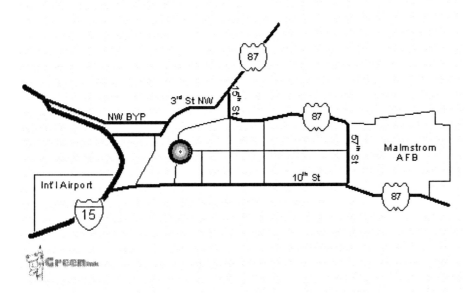

NAME: **The Elusive Moose**
LOCATION: 1369 Highway 93 North, Victor MT 59875
TYPE: Indoor Range
COST: Free
DIRECTIONS: The Elusive Moose is located south of Missoula Montana just north of the Sheafman Creek Corner and midway between Hamilton and Victor, MT. It is almost exactly 5 miles between the two towns. There is a very large arrow poking out of the ground on the edge of the parking lot and the building itself is well marked
DESCRIPTION: Indoor Range 14 Lanes / 30 Yards
At the Elusive Moose range, you can shoot in any kind of weather and after dark in the winter. Our indoor, 14 lane, 30 yard archery range is open all year round and available for use anytime during regular business hours. Business and range hours are 10-7 Tuesday through Friday and 10 - 5 on Saturday. The Elusive Moose is child friendly, the coffee is on and the weather is always nice in our indoor range.
CONTACT: 406-961-3991   Fax: 928-962-4530
             Web: http:theelusivemoose.com

Illustration- The Elusive Moose

The Elusive Moose
1369 Highway 93 North, Victor MT 59875

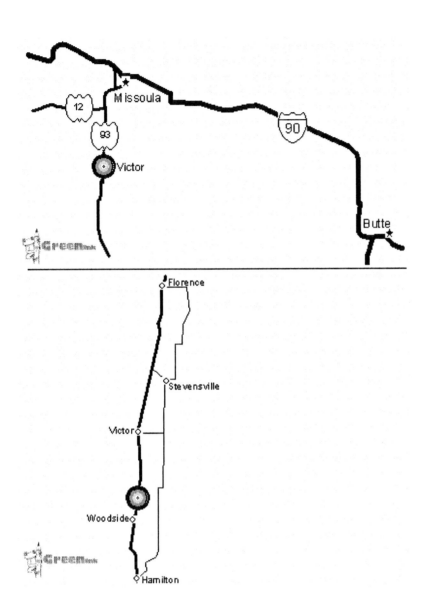

NAME: **Five Valleys Archery Club**
LOCATION: 1212 Longstaff St. Missoula MT 59801-3620
TYPE: Indoor Range & Outdoor Course
COST: $3.00 per hour.
DIRECTIONS: From I90 take N Orange St. exit South 1.3 miles. N Orange becomes Stephens Ave (US-93) 0.6 miles. Turn slight Right on Knowles St. .02 miles. Turn Left on Longstaff St. 0.1 miles.
DESCRIPTION: Range has 15 lanes up to 30 yards. Course has 35 3-D targets from 10 to 60 yards.
CONTACT: Paul Roush (406) 721-5537 montanasaltydog@hotmail.com

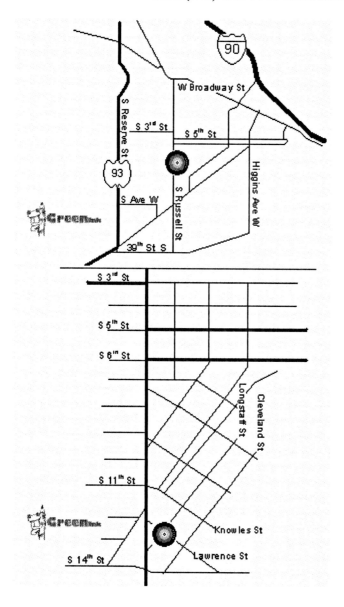

NAME: **Great Falls Archery Club**
LOCATION: Great Falls, MT
TYPE: 2 Outdoor Ranges – Members Only
COST: Call for price
DIRECTIONS: Call for address and directions
DESCRIPTION: 2 outdoor ranges
CONTACT: For information on how to join our club or pay yearly dues call Dave, 406-452-3238

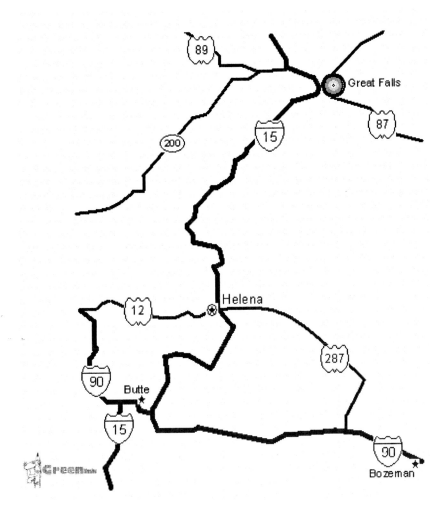

NAME: **Judith Basin Archery Club**
LOCATION: Judith Ranger District Stanford, MT 59479
TYPE: Indoor Range; Outdoor range
COST: Club Membership $30.00 Individual, $50.00 Family
                Ranges Free
DIRECTIONS: Outdoor range (Free to Public) 12 miles south of Stanford, MT on Dry
Wolfe Rd.
DESCRIPTION: Indoor Range 2 lanes, 20 yards; Outdoor Range 18 targets.
CONTACT: Scott Wildung (evenings) 406-566-2706

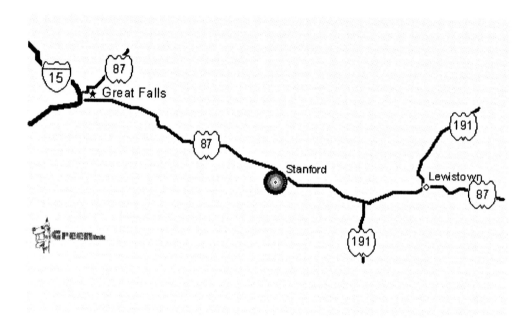

NAME: **Lewis and Clark Archers**
LOCATION: Helena, MT
TYPE: 2 Indoor Ranges and 1 Outdoor Course
COST: Free with an existing member. Annual membership fee: Youth: $25.00.
Single: $50.00 and a Family: $65.00
DIRECTIONS: Off of Broadwater Ave
DESCRIPTION: Local Archery Club. Welcome all archers. We have block indoor bales
and 12 lanes at 20 yards. (No broadheads allowed) Our outdoor bales are carpet and
burlap bales. Course has 28 targets with unmarked trails.
CONTACT: Katie Deyerle 406-431-9283
lewisandclarkarchers@gmail.com
http://www.lewisandclarkarchers.com

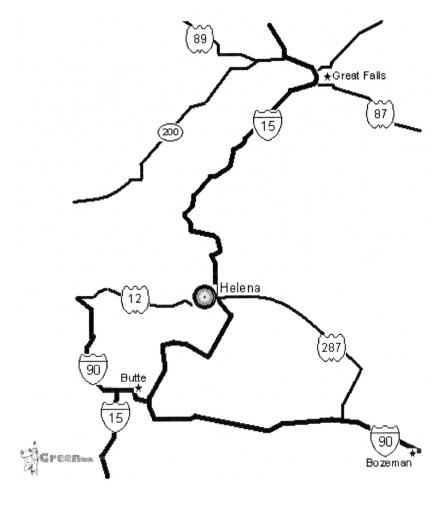

NAME: **Libby Archery Club**
LOCATION: Libby, MT
TYPE: Outdoor range
COST: $10 annually, $10 a month to shoot at the range they rent in the winter.
DIRECTIONS: Refer to map and call ahead for directions.
DESCRIPTION: Range is a covered shelter with targets set at 10, 20, 30 and 40 yards at our local rifle range. Indoor archery league are at rented space at the local bowling alley. Two shoots each year including 3-D with three courses of fifteen targets on each course with only traditional equipment. Families are welcome, there is camping, but no open fires and no running water on site. Games for the adults and kids including a balloon shoot for the kids and water bags shoot for kids and then one for adults. Several running targets including a flying pig, running deer, flying ducks and charging pig are used. Also a gopher courses round where the shooter tries to shoot as many gopher targets as possible in a set amount of time. The shoot has concessions and a catered dinner for minimal cost.

Both shoots are at awesome locations with some up and down walking. Boots or good hiking type shoes are best.
CONTACT: Tony Stephens 406-293-2072 libbyarcheryclubmt@yahoo.com.

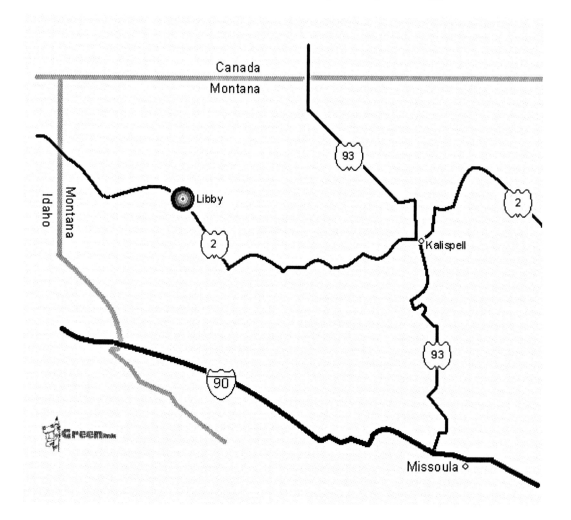

NAME: **Lone Pine State Park**
LOCATION: Kalispell MT
TYPE: Outdoor Range & Course
COST: $5.00 per vehicle Park fee.
DIRECTIONS: From I90 take US-93 approx 111 miles North. Turn Left on 10th St W for 0.5 miles. Right on 8th Ave W for 0.2 miles. Turn Left on 7th St W (MT-509) for 3.3 miles. Turn Left on Lone Pine Rd. and stay on it to the State Park.
DESCRIPTION: Open: April 15 - November 1. Park is disabled friendly with vault toilets.
CONTACT: 406-752-5501 www.stateparks.com/lone_pine.html or www.parkreservations.com/stateparks/montana/lonepine.htm

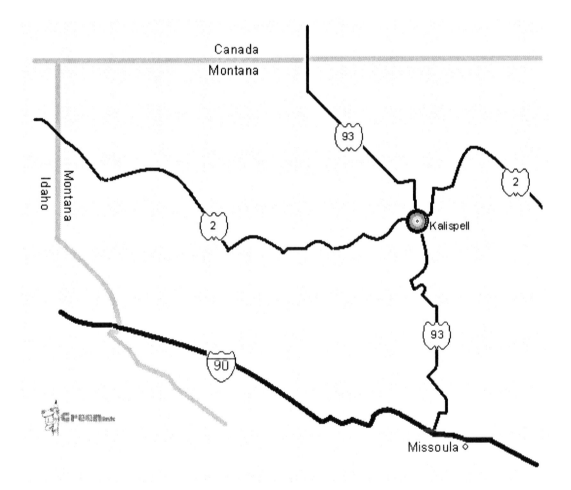

Lone Pine State Park
Kalispell MT

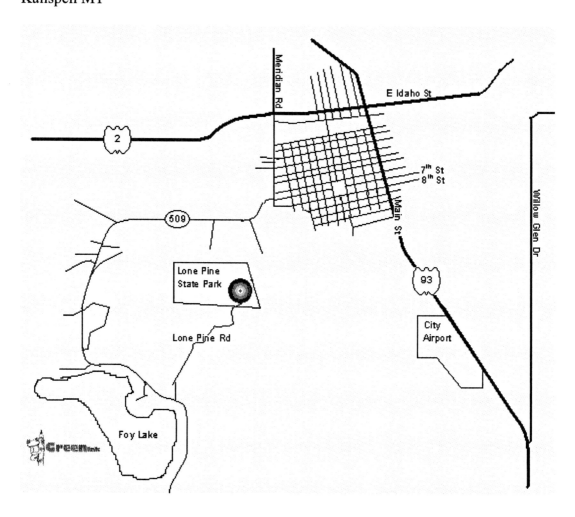

NAME: **Marias Valley Archers**
LOCATION: Shelby, MT
TYPE: Indoor & Outdoor Range
COST: Free with an existing member. Annual membership is $50.00 for individuals and $75.00 for a family.
DIRECTIONS: Just off of I15
DESCRIPTION: Indoor Range has 4 targets at 20 yards. Outdoor Range has 12 targets at 40 to 80 yards.
CONTACT: Mike Pederson 406-460-0649 mlpeder@3rivers.net

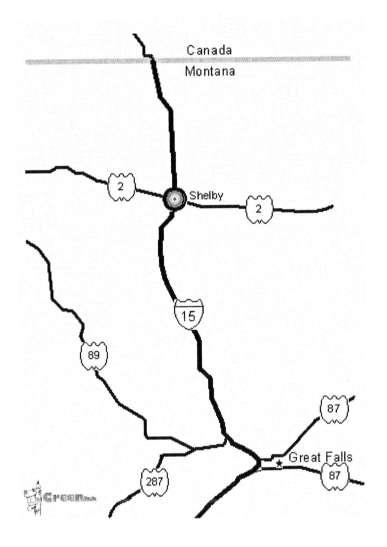

NAME: **Milk River Archery**
LOCATION: 1166 3rd St. N, Havre, MT 59501
TYPE: Outdoor 3-D Course
COST: Call for information
DIRECTIONS: From 2 head north on 7th Ave north; turn east on 1st St N; turn north on 11th Ave N; turn east on 3rd St N.
DESCRIPTION: 6 – 3D courses up to 40 yards.
CONTACT: 406-265-4927

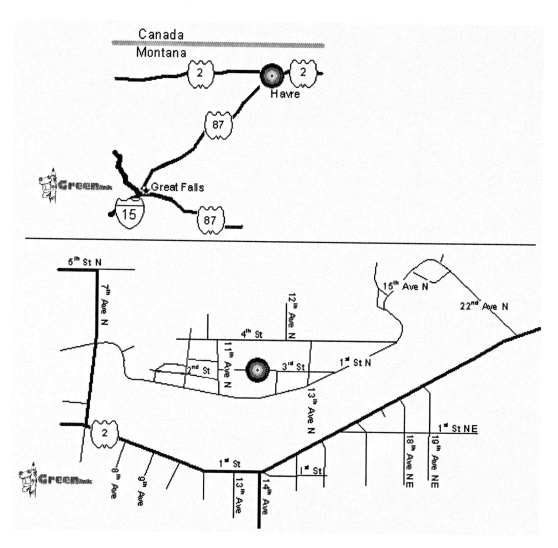

www.planetwildlife.net

NAME: **Rocky Mountain Archery**
LOCATION: 304 E Park St. Butte MT 59701
TYPE: Indoor Range
COST: $3.00 per day
DIRECTIONS: From I-15 take S Montana St. North. Turn Right on E Park St.
DESCRIPTION: Range is 12 lanes at 20 yards. Also ask about the Silver Bowl Archers Club located on Hwy 10. They boast 2 courses of 28 targets each; a 65 yard range and a 20 target 3-D Course. Annual membership is $50.00 individual & $65.00 Family.
CONTACT: 406-782-9400

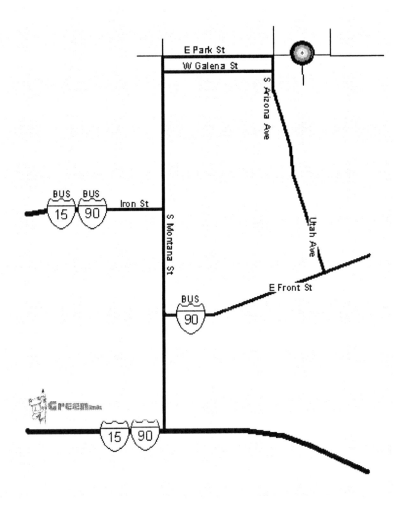

NAME: **Spirit Quest Archery**
LOCATION: 115 Rocky Cliff Rd. Kalispell MT
TYPE: Indoor Range & Indoor 3-D Course
COST: $5.00 per day for target Range and $8.00 per day for the Course
DIRECTIONS: From I-90 take US-93 107.3 miles North and Turn Left on Rocky Cliff Dr. 0.1 miles.
DESCRIPTION: Indoor Range is 13 lanes at 40 yards. 3-D is 20 targets at 40 yards including elevated platforms.
CONTACT: 406-756-5455

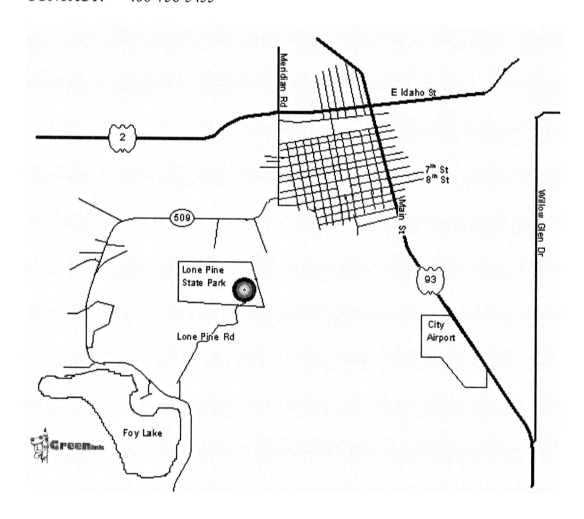

NAME: **Superior Archery, Inc.**
LOCATION: 1680 Lockwood Rd. Billings MT 59101
TYPE: Indoor & Outdoor Range
COST: $5.00 per day
DIRECTIONS: From I-90 take Bus. I-90 (MT-87) North. Take an immediate Right on Lockwood Rd.
DESCRIPTION: Indoor Range is 28 lanes from 10 to 20 yards. Outdoor Range is 10 lanes from 20 to 65 yards.
CONTACT: 406-245-0087

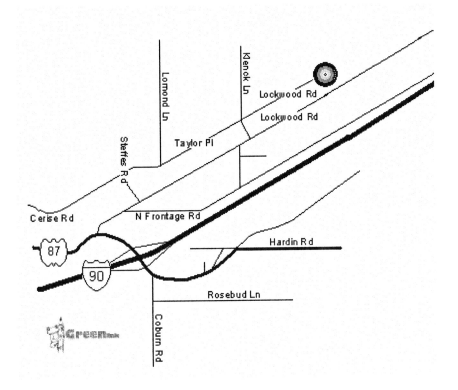

NAME: **Uncle Bob's Outdoors**
LOCATION: 11 Pierce Dr. Dillon MT 59725
TYPE: Indoor/Outdoor Range and Techno Hunt Video System
COST: Ranges are $3.00 per hour and $9.50 for Techno System.
DIRECTIONS: From I-15 take S Atlantic St Approx 1.2 miles. Turn Left on E Glendale St for three blocks. Turn Left on S Idaho St for 0.1 miles.
DESCRIPTION: Indoor Range is 3 lanes at 20 yards. Outdoor Range is 6 lanes from 20 to 40 yards. Techno System accommodates up to three people simultaneously. Discounts on per hour rate for additional shooters. $8.00 per hour for two and so on.
CONTACT: 406-683-2692

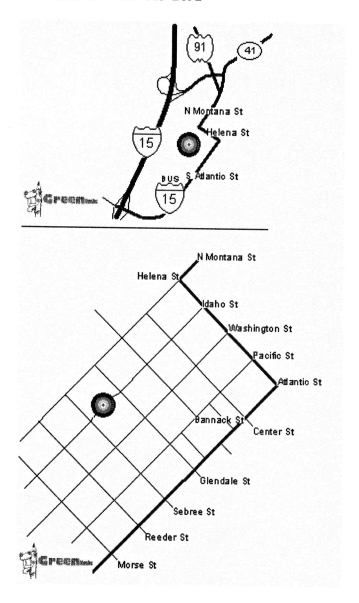

NAME: **Windy River Archery Club**
LOCATION: PO Box 863 Cut Bank MT 59427
TYPE: Outdoor Range
COST: $5.00 per day or $25.00 annual
DIRECTIONS: Refer to map and call for directions.
DESCRIPTION: Outdoor range at local gun range. Indoor range is under reconstruction.
CONTACT: Jim 406-873-2522

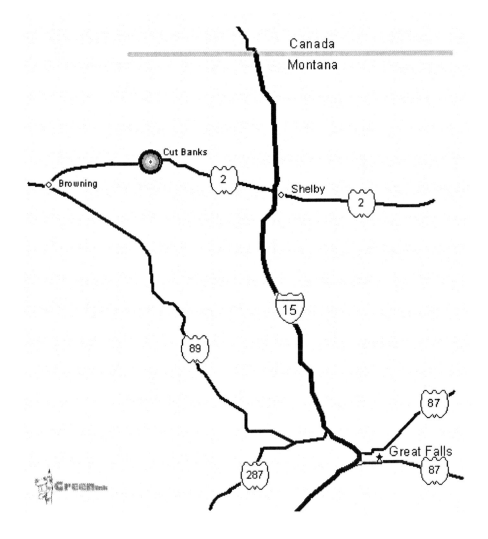

NAME: **Yellowstone Bowmen**
LOCATION: 909 Casa Linda Cir. Laurel MT 59044
TYPE: Indoor Range, Outdoor Range & 3-D Course
COST: Annual membership is $25.00 per individual or $35 per family
DIRECTIONS: From Billings take I-90 15.7 miles West. Turn right on S 1st Ave. 0.3 miles. Turn Left on W Main St (I-90 BR) 0.5 miles. Turn Right on 8th Ave. 0.6 miles. Turn Left on W 9th St. 0.1 miles.
DESCRIPTION: Indoor Range is 12 lanes at 20 yards. Outdoor is 80 lanes up to 80 yards and 60 targets on the 3-D course.
CONTACT: Flo Milliron 406-628-4727

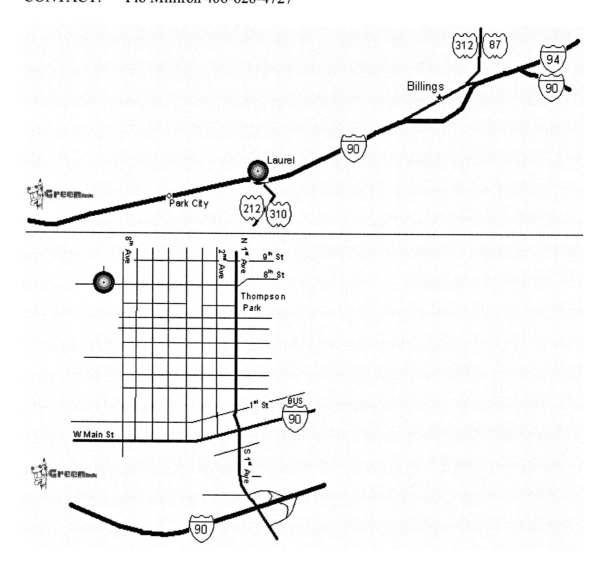

NAME: **Yellowstone Gateway Sports**
LOCATION: 21 Forkhorn Trl. Bozeman MT 59718-7597
TYPE: Indoor target & 3-D Range
COST: $6.00 per day or annual membership for $50.00 per individual or $80.00 per family.
DIRECTIONS: From I-90 take MT-85 South or US-191 West to Mt-85 North approx 7 miles.
DESCRIPTION: Range is 6 lanes up to 50 yards.
CONTACT: 406-586-2076

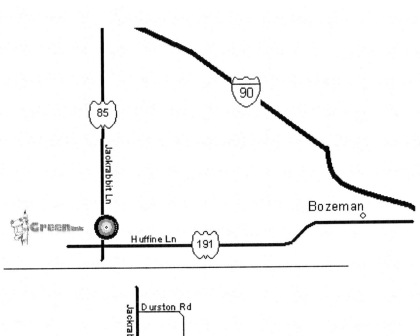

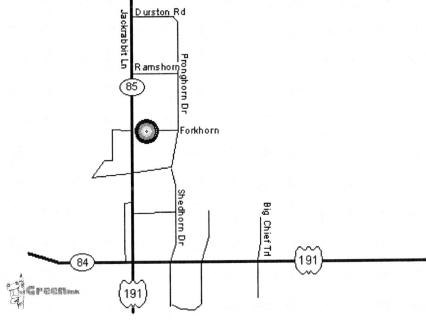

NAME: **Young Life Bowfest**
LOCATION: 3909 US Highway 93 N. Ste. 2 Stevensville, MT 59870-6490
TYPE: Kids club
COST: call for pricing
DIRECTIONS: Take US-93 South approx. 27 miles.
DESCRIPTION Young Life has been providing an outrageously fun, safe environment for kids since 1941. It is all around the country--in fact, all around the world--but it has finally made its way to the 'Root.
CONTACT: Andy Chidwick 406-546-7130 andy@bitterroot.younglife.org
www.bitterroot.younglife.org

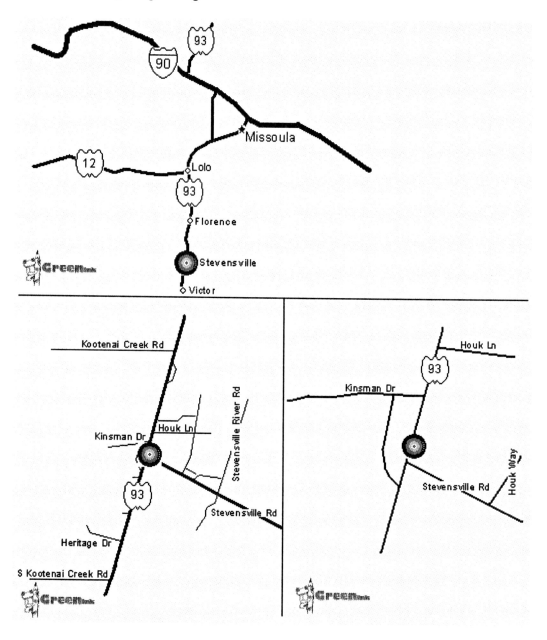

NEW MEXICO Locations

- ❏ Acoma Archery Club
- ❏ Action Sports Complex & Shooting Range
- ❏ Archers de Santa Fe
- ❏ Archery Hut
- ❏ Archery Shoppe
- ❏ Black Creek Archery
- ❏ Broke Bowhunters Club
- ❏ Four Corners Bow hunters
- ❏ Isleta Broken Arrow Archery Club
- ❏ Isleta Pueblo Archery Club
- ❏ Jinko Kyudojo
- ❏ Just Over the Back Archery Club
- ❏ Los Alamos Sportsman Club
- ❏ Mangus Bowmen Archery Club
- ❏ Navajo 3-D Archery
- ❏ New Mexico Roadrunners JOAD Archery Club
- ❏ NRGSC Archery
- ❏ Organ Mountain Bowmen
- ❏ S & J's Sporting Goods
- ❏ Sandia Crest Bowhunters Association
- ❏ San Juan Archers
- ❏ Sidney Paul Gordon Archery Range
- ❏ Willow Springs Archery Club
- ❏ Xpert Archery

NAME: **Acoma Archery Club**
LOCATION: Acoma NM
TYPE: Outdoor 3-D Range
COST: Free for visitors or $20 one time membership fee.
DIRECTIONS: Refer to map and call for location of Range
DESCRIPTION: This club sets up and removes 3-D targets on weekends. Call ahead of time for location. All profits go to youth programs and other community support.
CONTACT: Randal Torivio 505-552-7660 or 505-269-5801

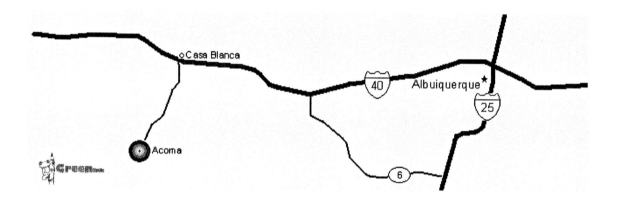

NAME: **Action Sports Complex & Shooting Range**
LOCATION: 314 North Happy Valley Road (State Highway 52A),
               2.5 miles north of Happy Valley Carlsbad, NM
TYPE: Outdoor Range
COST: Free to the Public
DIRECTIONS: This 645 acre recreation area is located at 314 North Happy Valley
Road, which is 2.5 miles north of Happy Valley on the Truck By-Pass.
DESCRIPTION: Included are four trap ranges, a pistol range, small and large bore rifle
ranges, silhouette rifle and pistol ranges, muzzle loaders range, archery range, cross-wind
runways for radio controlled model airplanes, and Yucca Flats Raceway - a competition
go-cart track.
CONTACT: Cavern City Bow Club
901 N. Canal, St., Suite 724, Carlsbad, NM 88220
Larry Clements - President, (575) 885-0159, l.clements@zianet.com
Tom Thompson - Secretary/Board of Directors, (575) 677-5128
Eddie Tabor - (575) 885-7737, eddietabor@zianet.com
www.cityofcarlsbadnm.com/parks_and_recreation/action_sports_complex

Illustration – Carlsbad Shooting Range

Action Sports Complex & Shooting Range
314 North Happy Valley Road (State Highway 52A), Carlsbad, NM

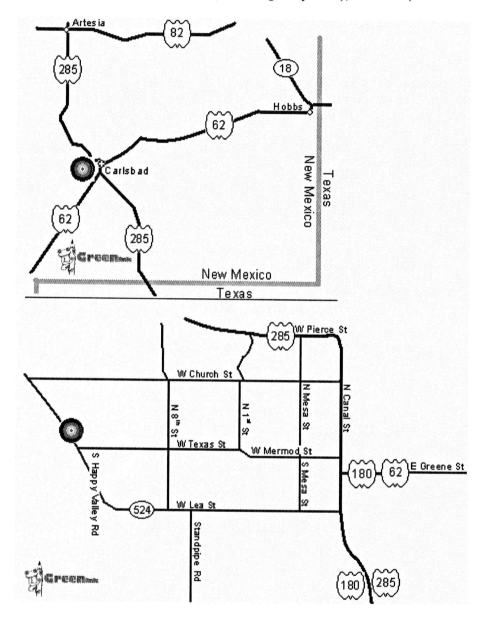

NAME: **Archers de Santa Fe**
LOCATION: Santa Fe NM
TYPE: Private outdoor range-outdoor course coming in spring
COST: Annual membership-Single $36.00-Family $43.00
DIRECTIONS: Call
DESCRIPTION: Range has 20, 30, 40, 50 & 60 yard targets; toilets and covered picnic area. Membership gives 24/7 access. Course will consist of 14 targets.
CONTACT: Mark Peck 505-490-0738 chrispower323@aol.com

Illustration - Taos Pueblo

Archers de Santa Fe
Santa Fe NM

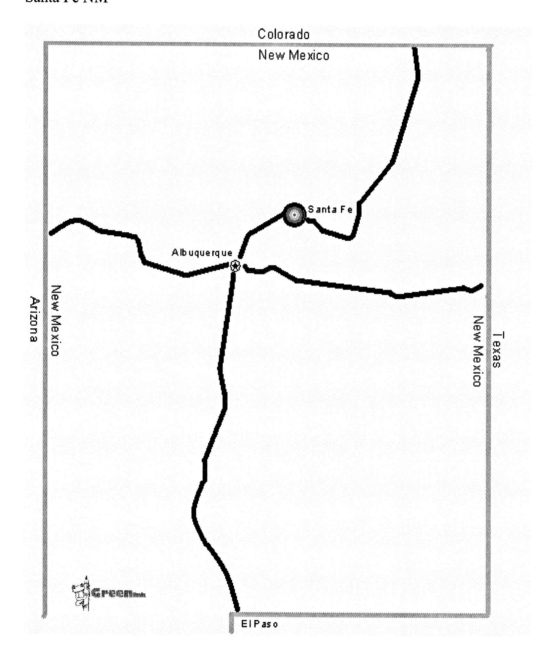

www.planetwildlife.net

NAME: **Archery Hut**
LOCATION: 1400 E Idaho Ave. Las Cruces NM 88001
TYPE: Indoor range and Electronic Shooting System
COST: $4.00 per hour
DIRECTIONS: From I10 take E University Ave (NM-101) East 0.6 miles: From I15 take NM-101 West 0.6miles. Take S Espina St. North 1.1 miles. Turn Right on E Idaho Ave. 0.2 miles. Recently we renovated and expanded the shop for a shor and long shooting Range as well as the Dart Electronic Shooting System. Open 1-6 PM.
DESCRIPTION: Range is 8 lanes at 20 yards.
CONTACT: 505-522-7468 or 888-663-1445 archeryhut@zianet.com

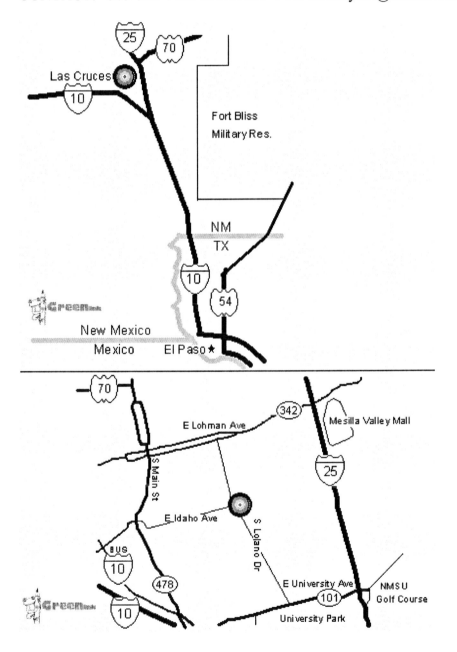

NAME: **Archery Shoppe**
LOCATION: 2110 Carlisle Blvd. NE Albuquerque NM 78110-3810
TYPE: Indoor Range
COST: $2.00 for 15 Min. $4.00 for 30 Min. $6.00 for 1 hr. or $10.00 all day.
DIRECTIONS: From I40 turn South on Carlisle Blvd.
DESCRIPTION: This location will RENT you a BOW for $10.00 and that includes your all day, come and go, pass.
CONTACT: 505-878-9768

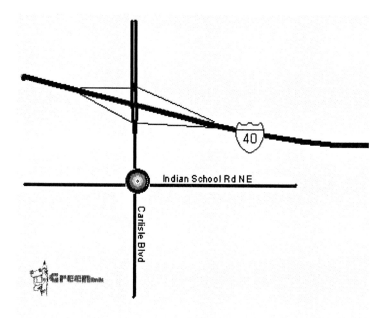

NAME: **Black Creek Archery**
LOCATION: PO Box 425, Navajo, NM 87328 (on reservation)
TYPE: Outdoor range and course 3D targets
COST: $5.00 /day
DIRECTIONS: Call for directions to course
DESCRIPTION: Practice Range 6 lanes at 20-60 yards. Course 20- 3D targets Course open during good weather.
CONTACT: 505-777-2630

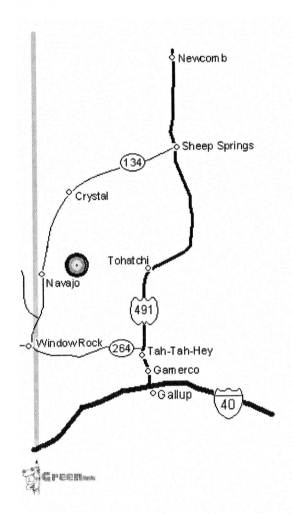

NAME: **Broke Bowhunters Club**
LOCATION: Los Lunas NM
TYPE: Private hunting and tournament club
COST: Free membership
DIRECTIONS: Refer to map and call ahead for directions.
DESCRIPTION: Meets each Wednesday
CONTACT: Ed LooseArrow (505)720-3291 pinkpigs17@msn.com

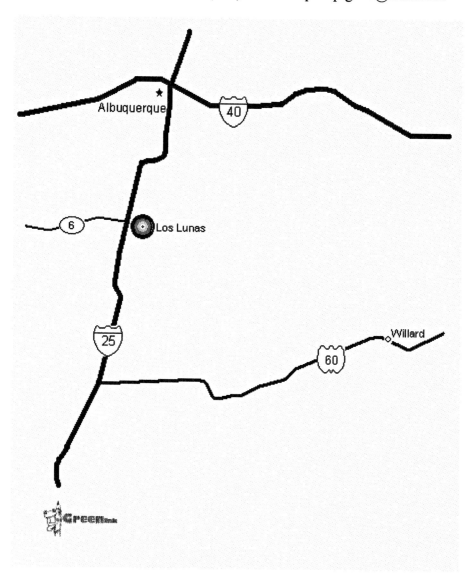

NAME: **Four Corners Bow hunters**
LOCATION: Flora Vista NM
TYPE: outdoor range
COST: $15 per day
DIRECTIONS: Refer to map and call ahead for directions.
DESCRIPTION: Targets are set up and removed every Tuesday only
CONTACT: 505-793-0295 dustyperry@peoplepc.com

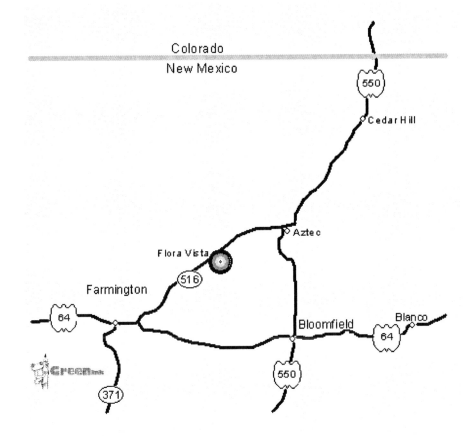

NAME: **Isleta Broken Arrow Archery Club**
LOCATION: Isleta NM
TYPE: Outdoor Range
COST: Free to members; $25.00 for events
DIRECTIONS: Refer to map and call ahead for directions.
DESCRIPTION: Range is set up and removed at various times and locations
CONTACT: Justin Lente 505-869-0098

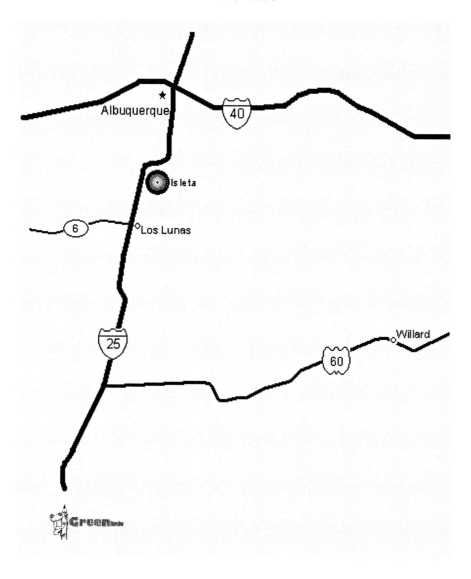

NAME: **Isleta Pueblo Archery Club**
LOCATION: Isleta Pueblo NM
TYPE: Outdoor course on reservation
COST: Free to members; no membership fees
DIRECTIONS: Refer to map and call ahead for directions.
DESCRIPTION: Course is set up and removed at various times and locations.
CONTACT: Eugene Jiron (505)869-6023 or 363-6835

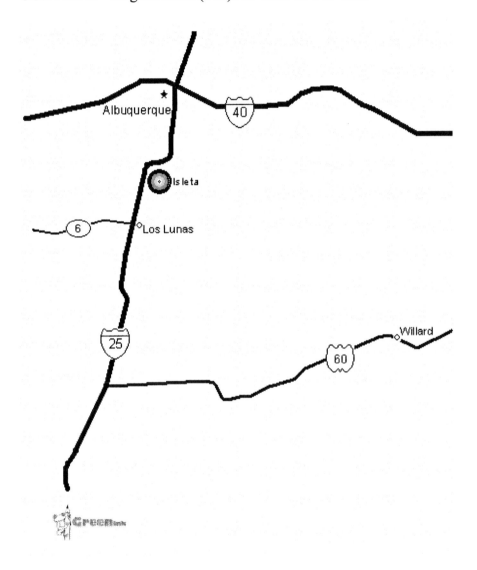

NAME: **Jinko Kyudojo**
LOCATION: Santa Fe NM
TYPE: Indoor Range
COST: Call
DIRECTIONS: Refer to map and call ahead for directions.
DESCRIPTION: **Kyudo**, the Way of the Bow, is one of the oldest arts in the Japanese tradition of contemplative warriorship. Working with the precision of the form, a natural process gradually unfolds in which the practitioner has the opportunity to see his or her mind at the moment of the arrow's release. This distinguishes Kyudo from sports archery where competition to hit the target is the goal. Kyudo is a long-term discipline of synchronizing body and mind to ultimately connect with one's warrior heart.

For every student, the Kyudo experience carries its own special meaning. Some encounter their fear of confrontation, others, the difficulty in letting go. For many, Kyudo is a way of relieving stress by quieting their mind as they focus completely on the meditative process of shooting the "ya" or arrow. Zen Archery is a way to polish the mind and manifest natural dignity.

Illustration – Jinko Kyudojo

We offer regular weekly Kyudo classes in meditation, equipment care and several elaborate archery forms. They are taught in a simple and thoughtful way to ensure that the student will become adept in the Kyudo forms and well-grounded in the principles from which they derive.

"Kyudo is not just about drawing the bow and the shichido, seven coordinations are not all that are being asked of you. Rather, within this practice, to acquire a good heart, and to achieve dignity in one's shooting is what is sought."

CONTACT: 505-780-2743 Info@jinkokyudojo.com www.jinkokyudojo.com

Jinko Kyudojo
Santa Fe NM

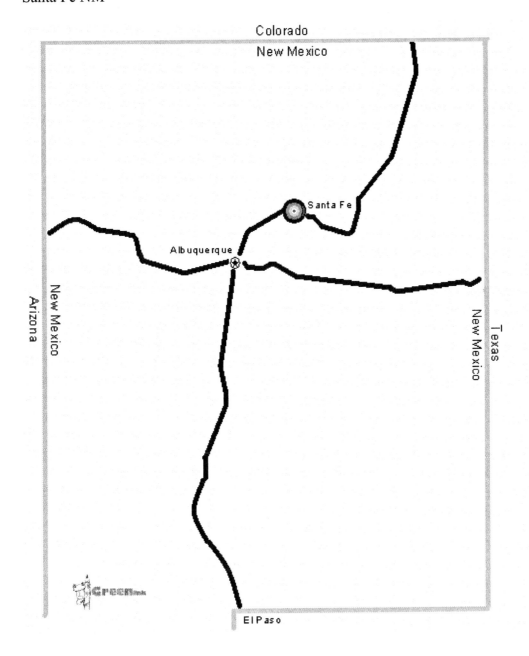

NAME: **Los Alamos Sportsman Club**
LOCATION: Los Alamos NM
TYPE: Outdoor Range-Private
COST: Annual membership is $84.00
DIRECTIONS: Refer to map and call for directions.
DESCRIPTION: Call ahead of time for groups of 5 or more for daily use. Range is 7 lanes from 10 to 80 yards.
CONTACT: 505-661-8143

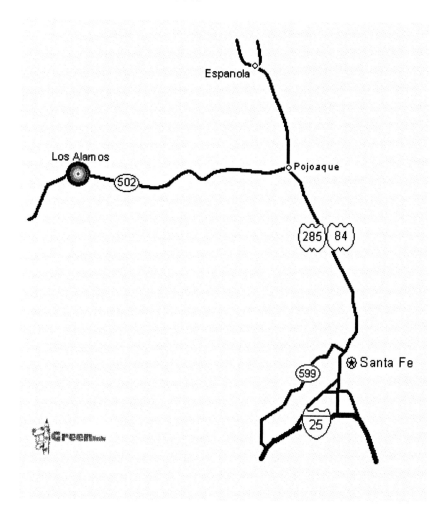

NAME: **Mangus Bowmen Archery Club**
LOCATION: Mimbres NM
TYPE: Outdoor Range
COST: Call
DIRECTIONS: Course is located at Ft. Bayard
DESCRIPTION: Course is set up and removed on various occasions.
CONTACT: Mike Scarsella 505-538-5211 or 505-313-1173
mscarsella@hotmail.com
www.mangusbowmen.com

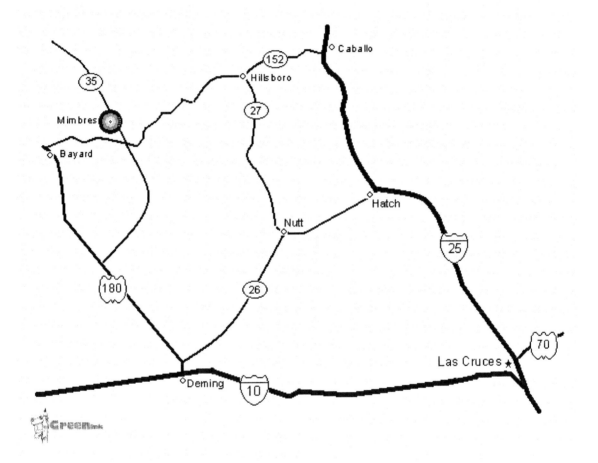

NAME: **Navajo 3-D Archery**
LOCATION: White Face Mountain Road, Tse Bonito, NM TYPE:
    Outdoor special event 3-D range.
COST: $1.00 per target. Average adult cost $20.00
DIRECTIONS: Starting from Gallup go north on Hwy 491 to the Edward O Plummer Interchange. Turn West on Hwy 264 or toward Window Rock, AZ. Near MP3 is the N-54 Intersection, also called the North P&M mine road. Go North to MP 6 and you will see "Whiteface Mt. Rd" sign, go north on this road. Once you pass the cattle guard you are on the N3-DA range.
DESCRIPTION: We use McKenzie 3-D targets and are moving to Rinehart targets. Unmarked distances in hunting scenarios. Dry camping on private land is available. Concession services are available depending on needs. N3DA has a primary function to raise funds for individuals. The efforts include tuitions assistance; travel costs for school, sports or personal development; emergency family expenses, etc. So we ask that individuals make a request in writing. Provide all the awards and help with the range set up. We rent out the targets at about $10 per day for one target (for a course of 20 that is about $200/day). N3DA is an affiliation of several Special Events clubs and archery groups. I have about 30 acres of land that we use to host events to promote archery.
CONTACT: Gordon Nez 505-371-5424 gordon_nez@hotmail.com   www.n3da.com

Illustration - Navajo 3-D Archery

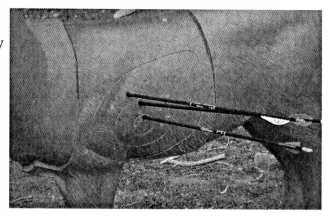

Navajo 3-D Archery
Bonito NM

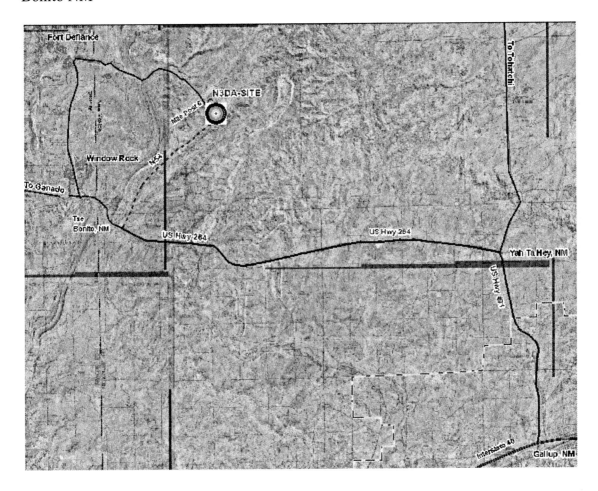

NAME: **New Mexico Roadrunners JOAD Archery Club**
LOCATION: Shooting At...Eagle Ridge Middle School, 800 Fruta Rd. Rio Rancho NM.
TYPE: Indoor & Outdoor Range
COST: $25 to $100 for package
DIRECTIONS: Refer to map and call for directions and hours or operation.
DESCRIPTION: We run a program based on the love of the sport of target archery, and character building. Indoor Range is 9 lanes from 5 to 18 yards. Outdoor range is 14 lanes from 10 to 90 yards.
CONTACT: Jenniffer Harvey 505-891-0923 jenniffer@nmarchery.org
www.nmarchery.org

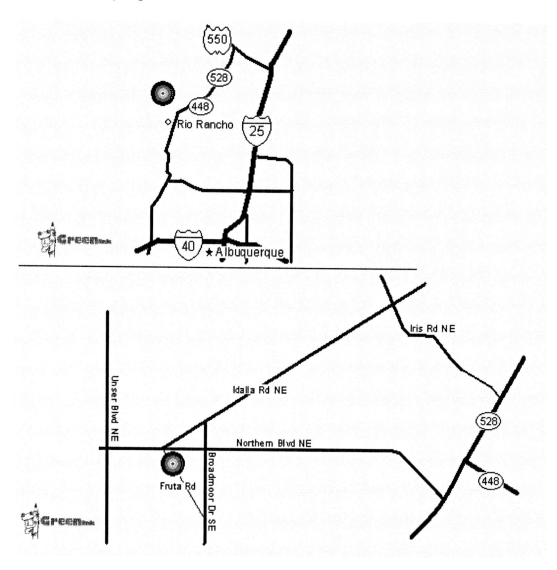

NAME: **NRGSC Archery**
LOCATION: Arroyo Alamo E. Santa Cruz, NM 87567
TYPE: Outdoor Ranges
COST: Memberships are $60 for two years per family
DIRECTIONS: Refer to map and call for directions.
DESCRIPTION: Northern Rio Grande Sportsmans club is a private, non-profit club in Northern New Mexico. The club maintains archery, pistol, and rifle ranges, sponsors competitions and training, and promotes the safe enjoyment of outdoor shooting and archery activities. Club facilities include a covered 400 yard rifle range, a 50 yard pistol range, a 200 yard rifle range for silhouette and high power, and extensive archery ranges. Club membership is opened to all U.S. citizens who are eligible to possess firearms and are willing to abide by club regulations.
CONTACT: Jason Gentry (505)929-7255 pfd51us@yahoo.com www.nrgsc.org

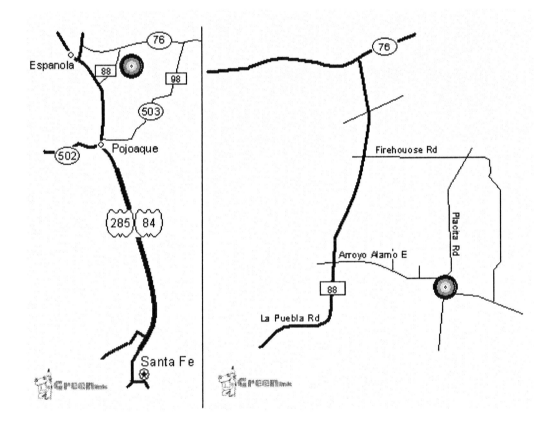

NAME: **Organ Mountain Bowmen**
LOCATION: Las Cruces, New Mexico
TYPE: Local Archery Club with indoor and outdoor facilities available.
COST: Yearly membership $15.00 individual - $25.00 family
DIRECTIONS: Refer to map and call ahead for directions.
DESCRIPTION: The OMB is a non-profit organization dedicated to promoting the family sport of archery. Indoor range at the local university and mobile targets are commonly set up at several outdoor locations.
CONTACT: Richard Von Wolff @ 505-527-1028,
omb@zianet.com, http://www.zianet.com/omb

Illustration - Organ Mountain Bowmen Indoor Range

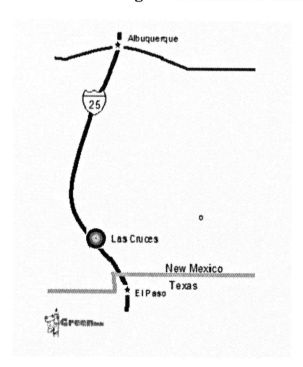

NAME: **S & J's Sporting Goods**
LOCATION: 544 Main St. NW, Los Lunas NM 87031
TYPE: Indoor range
COST: $5.00 per day
DIRECTIONS: From I25 take Main St. NW 1.3 miles East.
DESCRIPTION: Range has 11 lanes at 20 yards
CONTACT: 505-865-4241

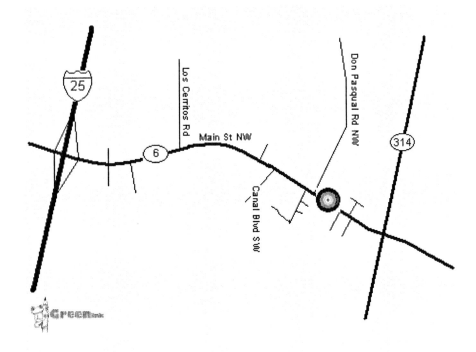

NAME: **Sandia Crest Bowhunters Association**
LOCATION: PO Box 11333 Albuquerque NM 87192
TYPE: Indoor range and Electronic Shooting System
COST: Outdoor 3-D Range
DIRECTIONS: Call or e-mail for directions.
DESCRIPTION: SCBA is a non-profit organization dedicated to the art of bowhunting and field archery. We maintain a full 28 target outdoor 3-D Range as well as long distance targets for the American Round enthusiasts. Membership applications are available at the archery shops in town or contact the association.
CONTACT: 505-980-3173 info@scbaarchery.org

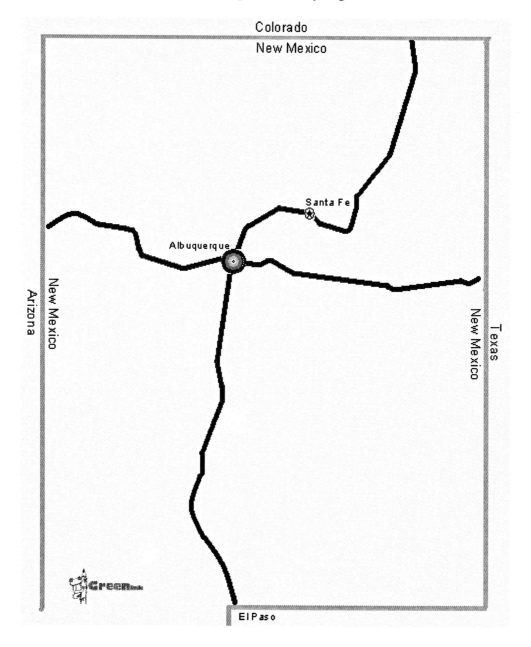

NAME: **San Juan Archers**
LOCATION: Farmington NM
TYPE: Private 32 acre range/course
COST: Free when accompanied by a member. $85 for family annual.
DIRECTIONS: Located at Pinion hills bypass & Glade Rd.
DESCRIPTION: Two 14 target courses with marked trails. Bathrooms and pavilion are located at range parking area.
CONTACT: Ruth Auckland 505-334-6929 or contact Xpert Archers also listed in this book.

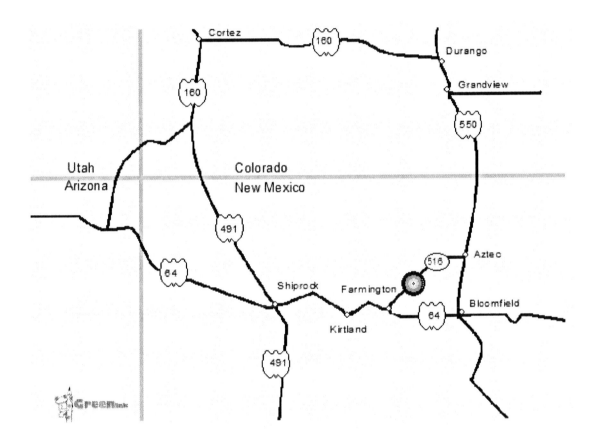

NAME: **Sidney Paul Gordon Archery Range**
LOCATION: 19 Rockcliff Rd. La Luz, NM 88337
TYPE: Outdoor Range
COST: $3.00 Per Day; Individual Pass - $38.00; Family Pass - $52.00;
Law Enforcement Family Pass - $30.00. (Seniors over 60 and County Employees receive a $5.00 discount on passes.) Pass allows unlimited visits to Range during normal hours
DIRECTIONS: (Located North of La Luz, New Mexico off Laborcita Canyon Road)
DESCRIPTION: 60 Yard Archery; Archery 3D Targets
CONTACT: 505-443-9006 http://co.otero.nm.us/MiscDept/shootrg.htm

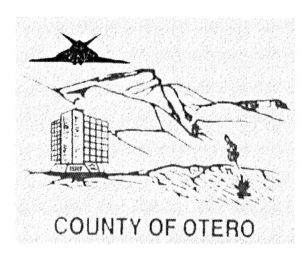

COUNTY OF OTERO

Illustration - Sidney Paul Gordon Archery Range

Sidney Paul Gordon Archery Range
19 Rockcliff Rd. La Luz, NM 88337

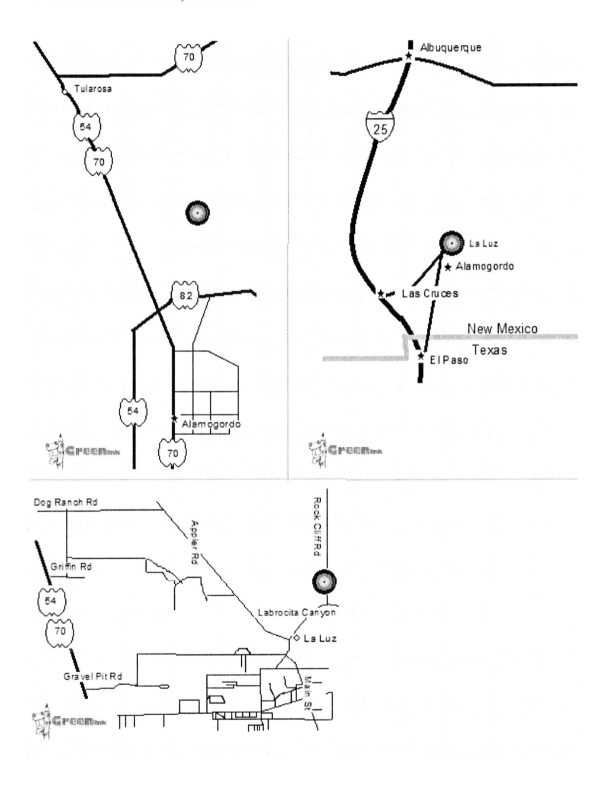

NAME: **Willow Springs Archery Club**
LOCATION: Raton NM
TYPE: Indoor range
COST: N/A at this time: Jan 2008
DIRECTIONS: Refer to map and call for directions
DESCRIPTION: Due to problems with the building, Willow Springs Archery Club is closed and will reopen when repairs can be completed.
CONTACT: Mike Brattain 505-445-1180 wsaclub@yahoo.com
www.willowspringsarchery.com/

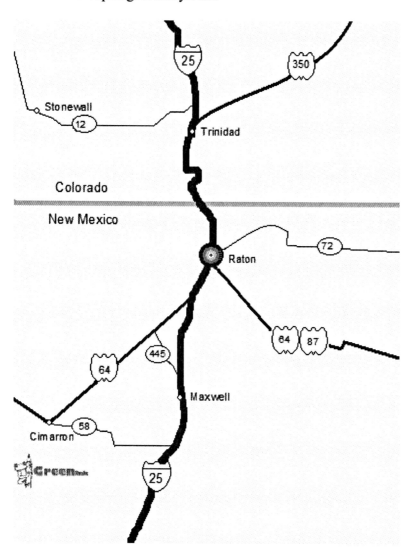

NAME: **Xpert Archery**
LOCATION: 5925 E Main St # B, Farmington, NM 87402-3023
TYPE: Indoor range
COST: $5.00 per hour
DIRECTIONS: Refer to map or call for directions.
DESCRIPTION: 10 lanes; 20 yards
CONTACT: 505-325-5544

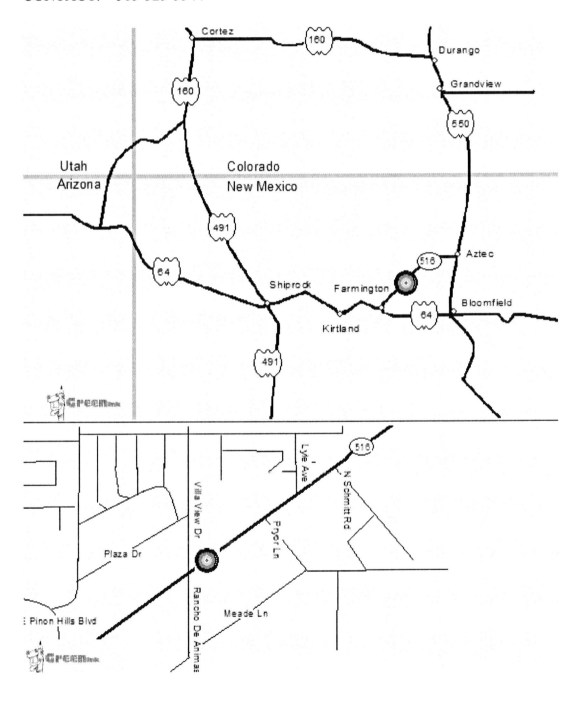

Safety Vest and Starburst string silencers provided by Mr. Big Bad Archery Fashions www.mrbigbad.com

UTAH Locations

- ☐ Cache Archers
- ☐ Cache Valley Public Shooting
- ☐ Deseret Peak Archery Park
- ☐ Hill Archers
- ☐ Humphries Archery
- ☐ Ibowhunt
- ☐ Jakes Archery
- ☐ Lee Kay Public Shooting Range
- ☐ Salt Lake Archery
- ☐ Timpanogos Archers
- ☐ TnT Archery
- ☐ TSI Outfitters
- ☐ Wilde Arrow

NAME: **Cache Archers**
LOCATION: P.O Box 3324 Logan Utah 84321
TYPE: Outdoor 3d range in Logan Canyon with 60 Rinehart targets, Indoor range
is located at the Cache Valley public shooting range
COST: $ 50.00 yearly membership
DIRECTIONS: Refer to map and call ahead for directions.
DESCRIPTION: We are a club made up of bowhunters and target shooters that try to
promote Archery to everyone we can. We have three seasons of circle leagues along with
indoor winter 3d league and year around youth leagues
CONTACT: Shawn Hansen 435-563-9601 sshansen@pcu.net

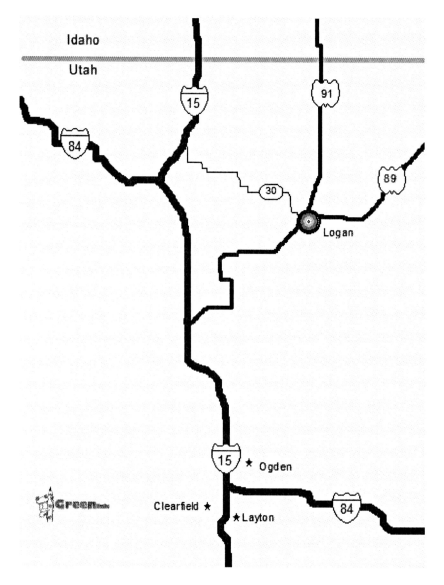

NAME: **Cache Valley Public Shooting**
LOCATION: 2851 West 200 North, Logan, UT 84321
TYPE: Outdoor & Indoor Range
COST: Public Access
DIRECTIONS: From I-15 take UT-30 approx. 15.6 miles East.
DESCRIPTION: 50-100 Yard Outdoor Rang and Indoor Range is 50 Foot.
CONTACT: 435-753-4600

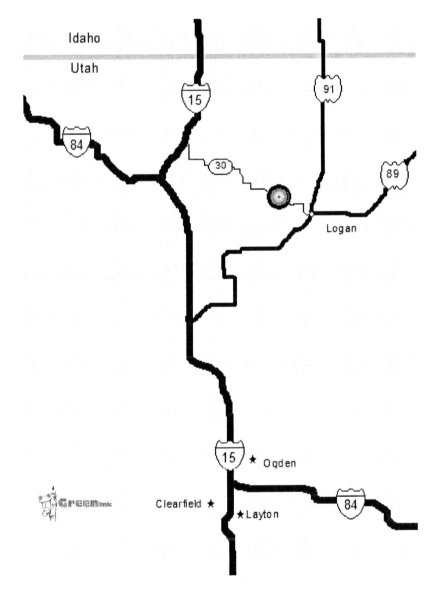

NAME: **Deseret Peak Archery Park**
LOCATION: 2930 W Hwy 112, Tooele UT
TYPE: Outdoor Range
COST: Non-members $10.00 & $8 for Members. Membership Due's $30 individual-$35 family
DIRECTIONS: The Deseret Peak Archery Range is home to tournaments, leagues and practices. Equipped with stable targets for your shooting convenience the archery park is open to the public year round. The archery park is open for events by appointment.
DESCRIPTION: Take I-80 West from SLC, take exit 99 to Tooele. Now traveling on SR 36. Continue past Lake Point. Before Stansbury Park turn right at street light SR 138. Proceed to Sheeplane and turn left. The Complex is at the corner of Sheeplane and SR 112
CONTACT: 435-843-4000/884-3410
http://www.deseretpeakcomplex.com/files/venues/archery.htm

Illustration - Deseret Peak Archery Park

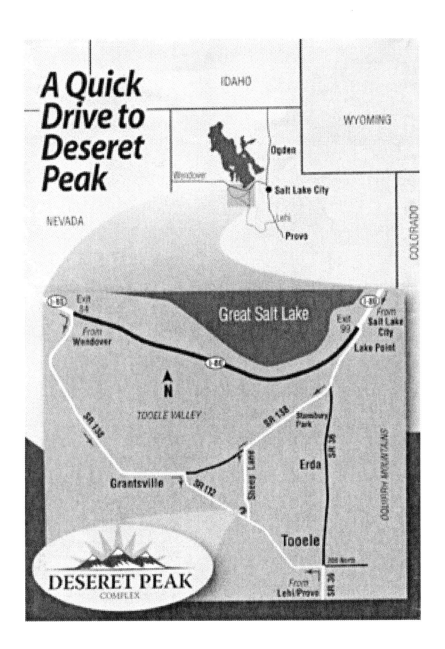

NAME: **Hill Archers**
LOCATION: Hill Air Force Base UT
TYPE: On military instillation
COST: Call
DIRECTIONS: Refer to map and call ahead for directions.
DESCRIPTION: Open to people with military base access only
CONTACT: Bob James 801-777-1995 robert.e.james@hill.af.mil

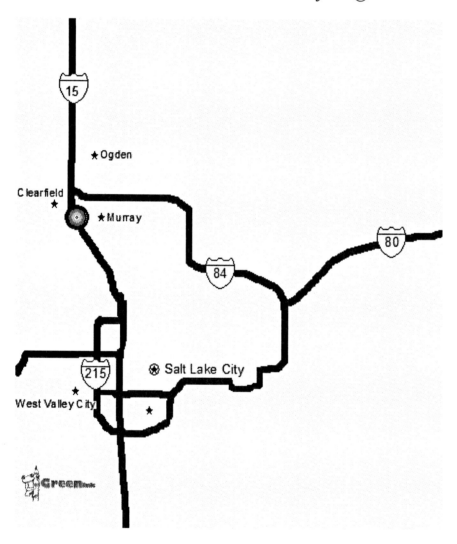

NAME: **Humphries Archery**
LOCATION: 42 West Main St. American Fork UT
TYPE: Indoor Range
COST: Public Access
DIRECTIONS: From I-15 take S 500 E (UT-180) North 0.8 miles. Turn Left on E State Rd (US-89) 0.8 miles to 42 W Main St.
DESCRIPTION: 20 Yards
CONTACT: 801-756-4750

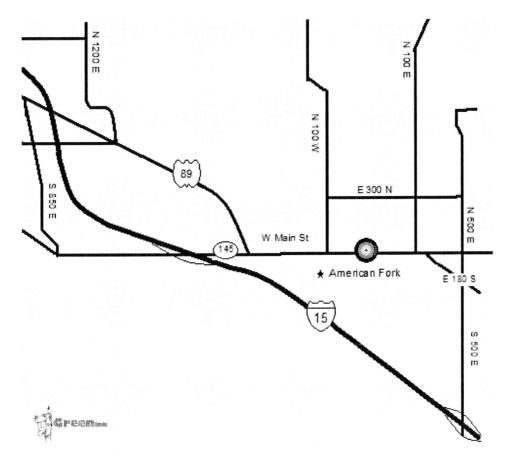

NAME: **Jakes Archery**
LOCATION: 765 S. Orem Blvd, Orem, UT 84058
TYPE: Indoor Range & Outdoor Course
COST: $5.00 per day for Range & $10.00 for equipment rental which includes per day fee.
DIRECTIONS: From I15 take W University Pkwy (UT-265) East 1.1 miles. Turn Left on S Main St. 0.6 miles. Turn Right on E 800 S 0.2 miles. Turn Left on S courtesy Way/S Oren Blvd. 0.1 miles.
DESCRIPTION: Range is 7 lanes at 20 yard range. Professional instruction available. Outdoor Course is 28 targets with a $60.00 annual membership.
CONTACT: 801-225-9202

NAME: **Lee Kay Public Shooting Range**
LOCATION: 6000 West 1200 South, Salt Lake City, UT 84128-6441
TYPE: Indoor Range
COST: Public Access $4.00 all day.
DIRECTIONS: From I-15 take W 2100 S (UT-201) West 3.8 miles. Take 56th W Exit (exit 11) 0.3 miles. Turn Right on S 5600 W (UT-172) 0.1 miles. Turn Left on W 2100 S (a frontage road) 0.3 miles.
DESCRIPTION: Range has 10, 20, 30, 40, 50 and 60 yard targets. Open 9–5.
CONTACT: 801-972-1326

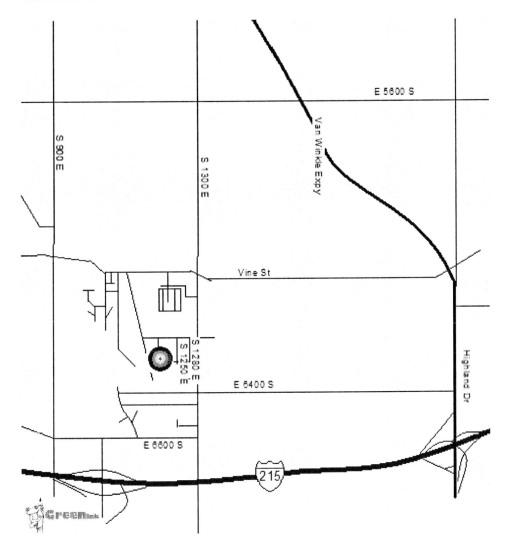

NAME: **Salt Lake Archery**
LOCATION: 1130 E Wilmington Ave. Salt Lake City UT 84106-2819
TYPE: Indoor range 18 lanes at 25 yards.
COST: Our regular shooting rate for people with their own equipment is $6.00 for all day. We have monthly passes for $30.00 and yearly passes for $300.00. If you need to rent equipment the cost for a recurve or Genesis bow, arrows and safety equipment is $5.00. There is no instruction included with the shooting or rental fee. Private lessons available by certified instructors and a full pro shop.
DIRECTIONS: From I80 take S 1300 E exit North bound and turn left on E Wilmington Ave.
DESCRIPTION: We challenge you to come in and try the DART Hunting Adventure. You can choose your favorite challenge from the following disks. $ You can have 1 to 4 people shooting in turn for the same cost.
CONTACT: 801-486-8242
www.saltlakearchery.com

NAME: **Timpanogos Archers**
LOCATION: PO Box 970833 Orem, UT 84097. Range is in Provo Canyon
TYPE: Outdoor Range and Courses, 3D course
COST: First visit free with an existing member. $80.00 first year family
membership (members must donated 15 hours of service) $65.00 annual renewal.
DIRECTIONS: Range is located in Provo Canyon
DESCRIPTION: 4 Courses 14 targets each, 3D course, 4 practice ranges. Up to 80 yards.
CONTACT: www.timparchers.com

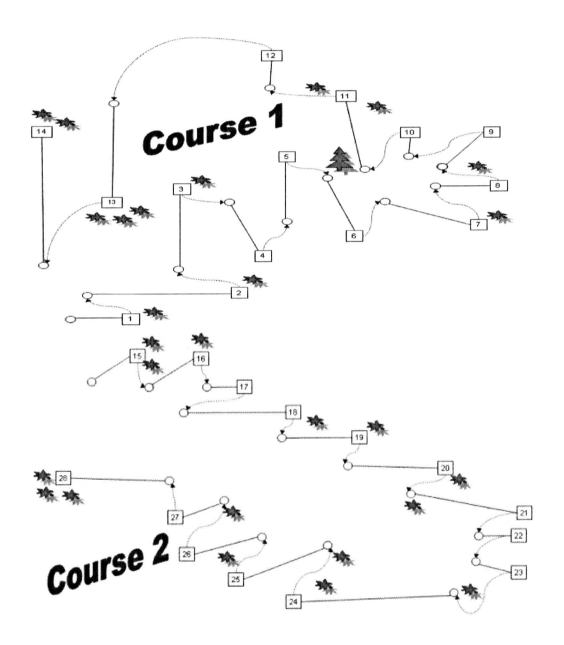

Timpanagos Archers
Orem, UT

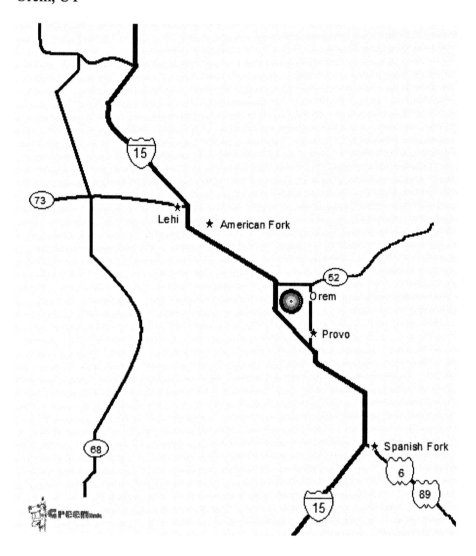

NAME: **TnT Archery**
LOCATION: 2299 Santa Clara Dr #C1, Santa Clara UT 84765
TYPE: Indoor Range
COST: $4.00 per hour
DIRECTIONS: From I-15 take S Bluff St. 2.8 miles West. Turn Left on W Sunset Blvd.
2.1 miles
DESCRIPTION: Indoor Range has 8 Lanes / 20 Yards
CONTACT: 435-656-9110

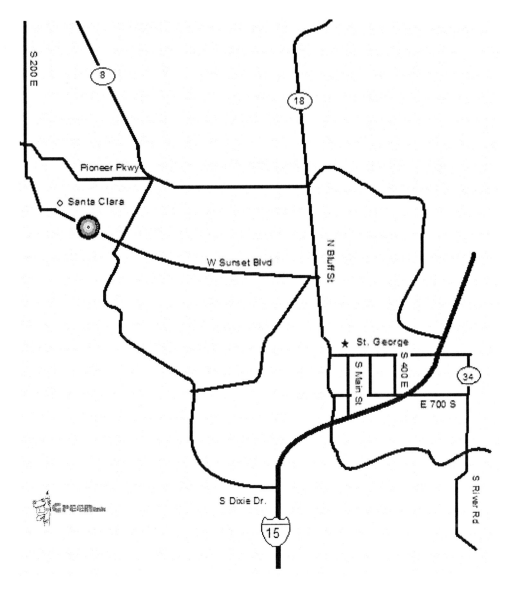

NAME: **TSI Outfitters**
LOCATION: 3245 West 7800 South, West Jordon, UT 84088-4508
TYPE: Indoor Range
COST: $7.50 per day or $10.00 per hour rental equipment including compounds.
DIRECTIONS: From I-15 take W 9000 S (UT-209) West 4.0 miles. Turn Right on
Bangerter Hwy. (UT-154) 1.4 miles. Turn Right on W 7800 S (UT-48) 0.3 miles.
DESCRIPTION: Indoor Range 24 Lanes / 30 Yards
               Indoor Course 15 Targets including tree stand
CONTACT: 801-260-0874   Fax: 801-260-0875
 Web: www.tsioutfitters.com   E-mail: info@tsioutfitters.com

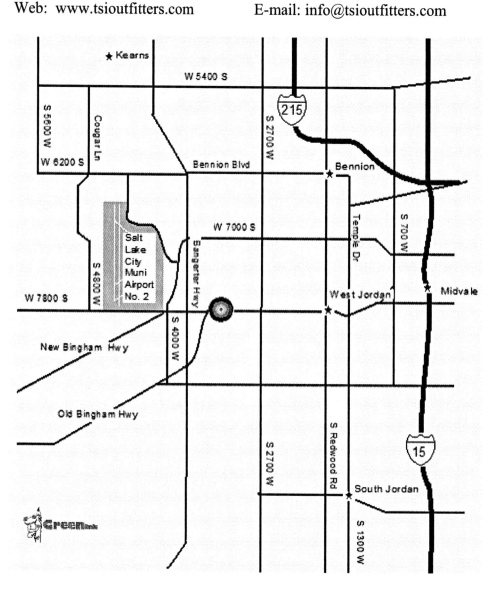

NAME: **Wilde Arrow**
LOCATION: 250 E Gentile St. Layton UT 84041
TYPE: Indoor Range & Techno Hunt
COST: $4.00 per half hour for the Range and $12.00 per half hour for Techno Hunt.
DIRECTIONS: From I-15 in North SLC, head East on take W Hill Field Rd (UT-232) West 0.1 miles. Turn Left (South) on N Main St (UT-126) 1.0 miles. Turn Left on E Gentile St (UT-109) 0.2 miles.
DESCRIPTION: Indoor Range has 3 Lanes / 20 Yards. Open from 12:00 noon Tue–Sat.
CONTACT: 801-546-0962

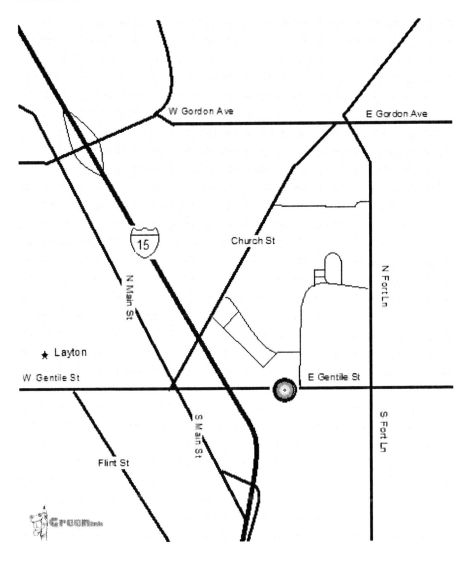

Advertising Space Available

WYOMING Locations

- ☐ Bighorn Bowhunters
- ☐ Buffalo Trap and Skeet
- ☐ Bullseye Archery
- ☐ Curt Gowdy State Park
- ☐ Cheyenne Field Archers Club
- ☐ Cambria Bow hunters
- ☐ Cheyenne North Community Park
- ☐ Cody Archery Club
- ☐ Gillette Gun Club
- ☐ Hell Hole Archers
- ☐ High Plains Archery Club
- ☐ Inya Kara Bowhunters
- ☐ L/C Bishop Sales
- ☐ Little Wind Archers of Fremont County
- ☐ Lost Arrow Archers
- ☐ Pronghorn Archery Club
- ☐ Rocky Mountain Discount Sports
- ☐ White Mountain Archery
- ☐ Wyoming Archery & Hunting Supply

NAME: **Bighorn Bowhunters**
LOCATION: P.O. Box163 Thermopolis WY 82443
TYPE: Indoor Range
COST: Annual membership is $20.00 plus $4.00 per night.
DIRECTIONS: Refer to map and call ahead for directions ant schedule.
DESCRIPTION: Club sets up both targets and 3-Ds on alternating nights at the local fairgrounds building.
CONTACT: http://www.angelfire.com/wy2/bighornbowhunter/index.html
Evenings: 307-864-2585 or d&mperry@directairnet.com

Thermopolis WY

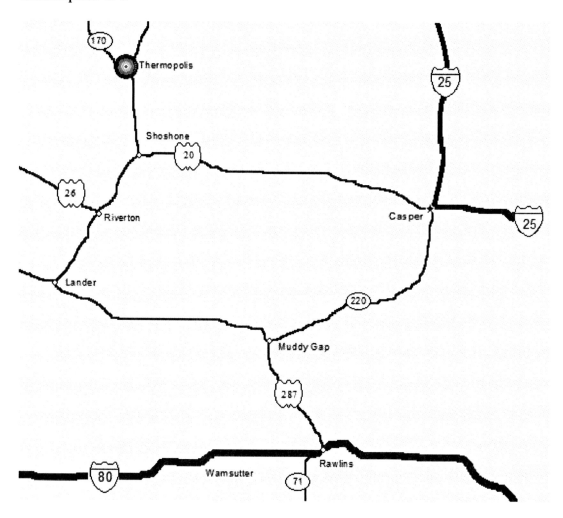

NAME: **Buffalo Trap and Skeet**
LOCATION: Contact **The Sports Lure** 66 South main St, Buffalo, WY 82834
TYPE: Outdoor Range
COST: Daily Key rental $2.00; Single Annual $15; Family Annual $25
DIRECTIONS: Contact The Sports Lure
DESCRIPTION: Archery Range located at gun range
CONTACT: 800-684-7682 http://www.sportslure.com/shootingranges.htm

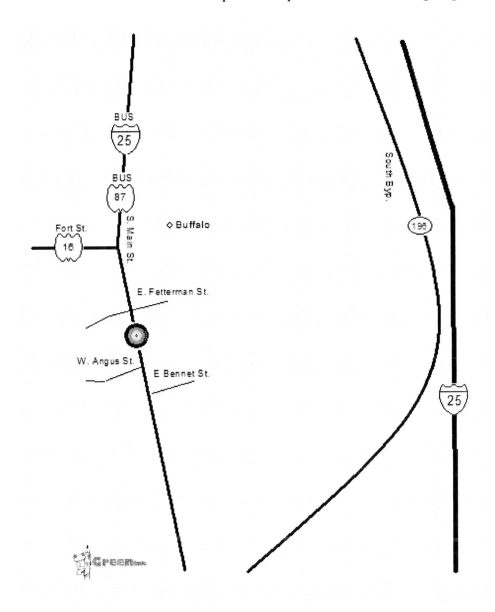

NAME: **Bullseye Archery**
LOCATION: 1212 Ridge Road, Cheyenne, WY 82001
TYPE: Indoor Range
COST: Free
DIRECTIONS: In shopping center on S. W. corner of Ridge and Lincolnway.
DESCRIPTION: Pro Shop with Indoor 20 yard Range.
CONTACT: Wilbur 307-637-7498

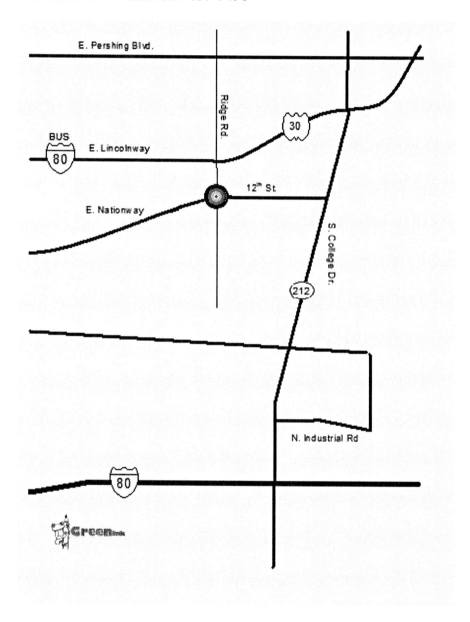

NAME: **Curt Gowdy State Park**
LOCATION: Curt Gowdy State Park
             1319 Hynds Lodge Road, Cheyenne WY 82009
TYPE: Public
COST: Park Fee; Resident $2.00; Non-Resident $4.00
             A donations box is also located at end of the Archery Course.
DIRECTIONS: If approaching from Cheyenne, turn onto Happy Jack Road (WY-210) traveling West 23.8 Miles from I25. If approaching from Laramie, turn onto Happy Jack Road (hwy 210) traveling East 13.1 Miles from I80. Enter Curt Gowdy State Park via Granite Springs Road and travel 1 Mile to Park entrance. Stay right and proceed approximately ¼ mile beyond park entrance gate; take the first available right hand turn and find parking. An outdoors-persons extravaganza parking, toilets picnicking camping mountain biking hiking horseback riding water sports, even a c store/ fire wood store The Archery Course is on the mountain just north of the lake inlet.
Park Map: http://wyoparks.state.wy.us/Parks/CurtGowdy/CurtGowdy.pdf
DESCRIPTION: This course consists of 28 targets. Each target consists of circle targets and or an animal target on excelsior bales. A moderate strength person may take as long as 3 hours to walk this often steep course, bring water bring snacks or even a picnic.
CONTACT: 307-632-7946

Illustration Deer on Curt Gowdy Course

Curt Gowdy State Park
1319 Hynds Lodge Rd
Cheyenne WY 82009-9004

NAME: **Cheyenne Field Archers Club**
LOCATION: Cheyenne WY
TYPE: Private club. Indoor Range
COST: $100 One Time Membership Fee: $50 annual Fee
DIRECTIONS: CALL
DESCRIPTION: Indoor Range – Members Only; 40 yards and 10 lanes
CONTACT: (307)638-9951

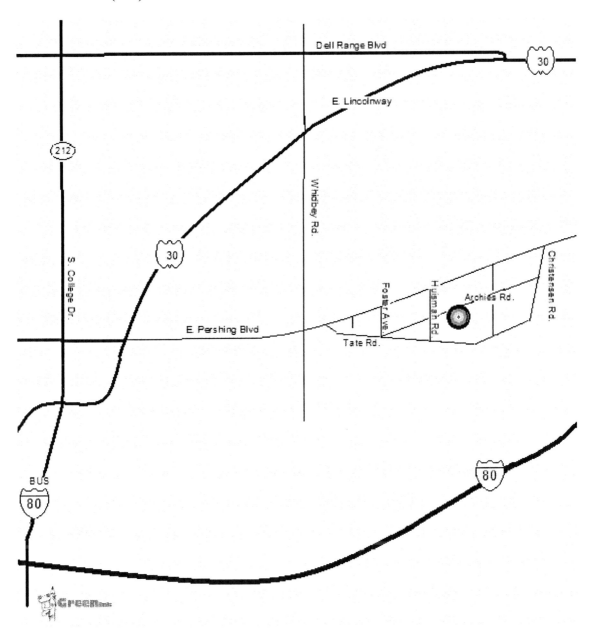

NAME: **Cambria Bow hunters**
LOCATION: Newcastle WY
TYPE: 24 lane Indoor Range & 28 Target field course
COST: Annual $25 individual $35 family
DIRECTIONS: Refer to map and call ahead for directions.
DESCRIPTION: We have one of the most active clubs in Wyoming established in April, 1978 with 10 members. Cambria Bowhunters now has almost 50 Family Membership's and growing. We have a 24 lane Indoor Range Sanctioned and Insured by the NFAA. Also a 28 Target field course, Guarantied to stop any Arrow also Sanctioned and Insured. Both courses are available 24 hours a day all year round with payed Membership. We try to keep our membership affordable so you and the whole family can have fun. Cambria Bowhunters are affiliated Member of the NFAA, WSAA and BOW.
CONTACT: Bryan McVay 746-4532; Jim Buchanan 746-3455; Jill Zerbst -746-9394

Illustration- Cambria Bowhunters 1

Illustration- Cambria Bowhunters 2

Illustration- Cambria Bowhunters 3

Cambria Bow hunters
Newcastle WY

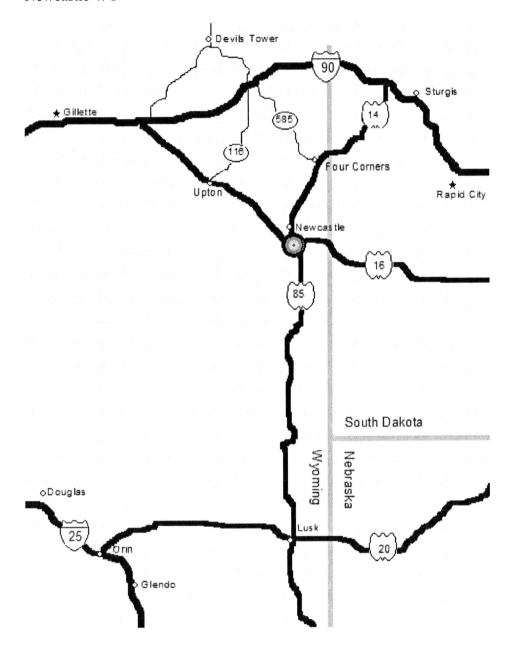

NAME: **Cheyenne North Community Park**
LOCATION: Ridge Road, Cheyenne, WY
TYPE: Outdoor Public Range
COST: Free
DIRECTIONS: next to soccer park off of Ridge Road
DESCRIPTION: Burlap animal targets on Bales
CONTACT: 307- 638-4356

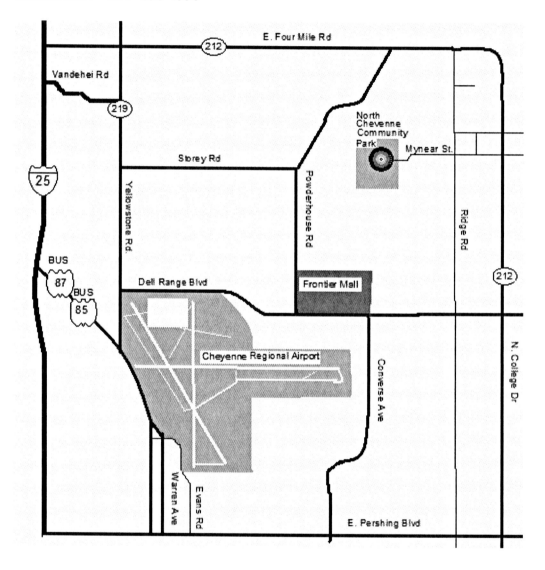

www.planetwildlife.net

NAME: **Cody Archery Club**
LOCATION: 356 W Yellowstone Ave. Cody, WY 82414
TYPE: Outdoor Range and 3-D Course
COST: Annual membership is $15.00 for an individual; $25.00 for a family and $250.00 for a lifetime membership.
DIRECTIONS: 6 miles east of Cody airport on Greybull Hwy 14
DESCRIPTION: This club uses several local indoor ranges during the winter and has an outdoor course for summer months. They have three 14 target Courses. This includes a small range and a clubhouse.
CONTACT: Zack Baker, evenings 307-587-4624

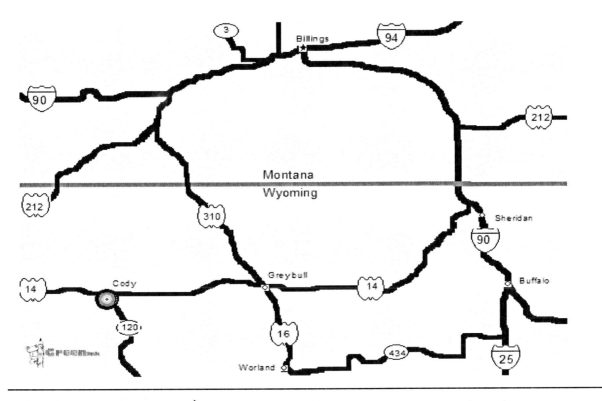

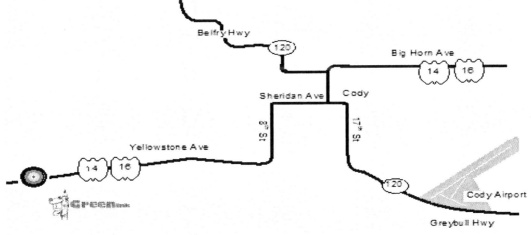

NAME: **Gillette Gun Club**
LOCATION: 52 Garner Lake Rd, Gillette, WY 82716
TYPE: Outdoor Range
COST: 2008 Annual Membership are on sale now at the Gun Club,
Gun Traders and Rocky Mountain Sports
DIRECTIONS: From I -90 take 14 North, cross the railroad tracks to E Warlow Dr; turn
west; turn north onto Hancoum Rd; turn east on Garner Lake rd.
DESCRIPTION: The club also has an archery range that has targets ranging from 20 to
60 yards
CONTACT: 307-682-9984 www.gillettegunclub.com

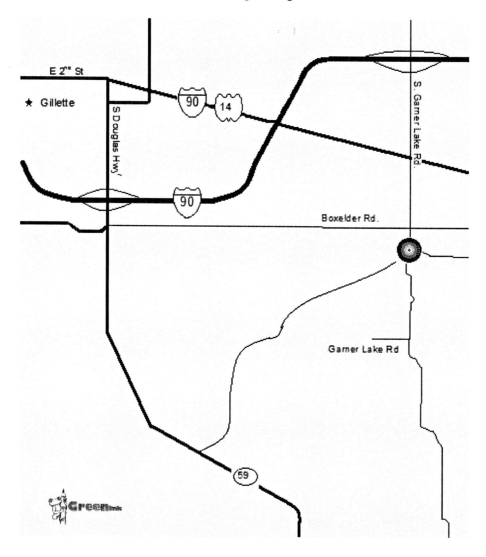

NAME: **Hell Hole Archers**
LOCATION: Big Piney WY
TYPE: Private Indoor Range
COST: Annual membership is $35.00 per individual and $55.00 per family.
DIRECTIONS: Refer to map and cal ahead for directions and schedule.
DESCRIPTION: Range is used for 12 weeks out of the year Feb. - Apr. including targets, 3-D targets and even a Dart System. Club participates in shoots during the summer months including BBQs and prizes. Range may be available at other times for members.
CONTACT: Preston Dhell 307-260-8810

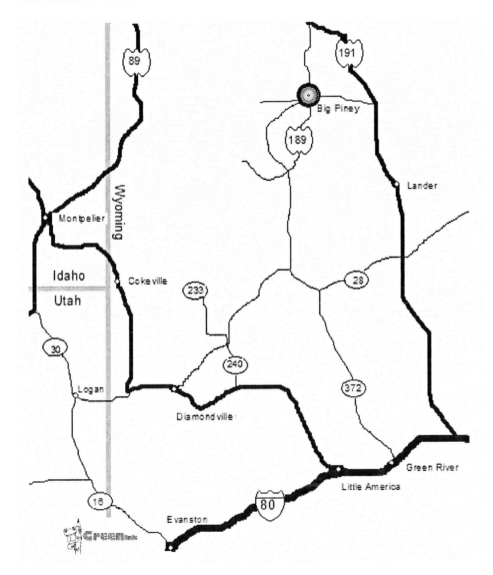

NAME: **High Plains Archery Club**

LOCATION: 209 South Cedar Street, Laramie, WY 82072

TYPE: Indoor Range

COST: $3.00 first time, Call or visit for annual membership.

DIRECTIONS: From West bound I-80 take Hwy 287 North to 130 West to S Cedar St South. From East bound I-80 take Hwy 130 East to S Cedar St. South.

DESCRIPTION: Range is 7 lanes at 30 yards. Their low membership rates provide you with 24 hour access, and the chance to participate in leagues on Monday and Wednesday evenings. If you are into Target archery, Hunting, or just want to kill some time, High plains is the place for you!!!

CONTACT: Stop by on Wednesday around 7:00 pm. and get signed up. 307-742-2965

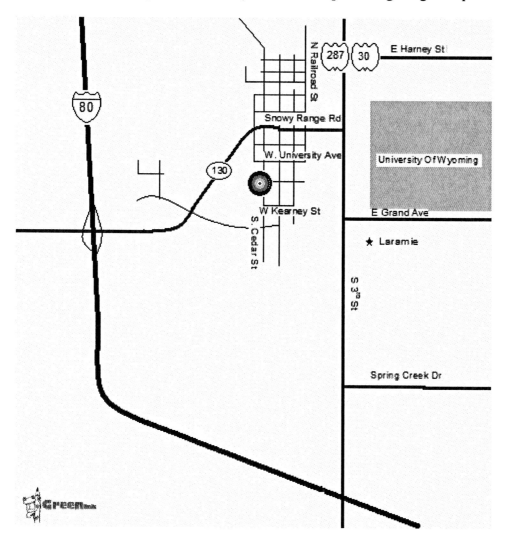

NAME: **Inyan Kara Bowhunters**
LOCATION: P.O. Box 403 Upton, WY 82730
TYPE: Public Outdoor Range
COST: Free to the public.
DIRECTIONS: Range is located 1.5 miles North of Upton on Hwy 116. Use the same gate as the Cedar Pines Country Club.
DESCRIPTION: Usually open from 7:00 am to dark.
CONTACT: Phone: 307-468-2647 country club # 307-468-2847

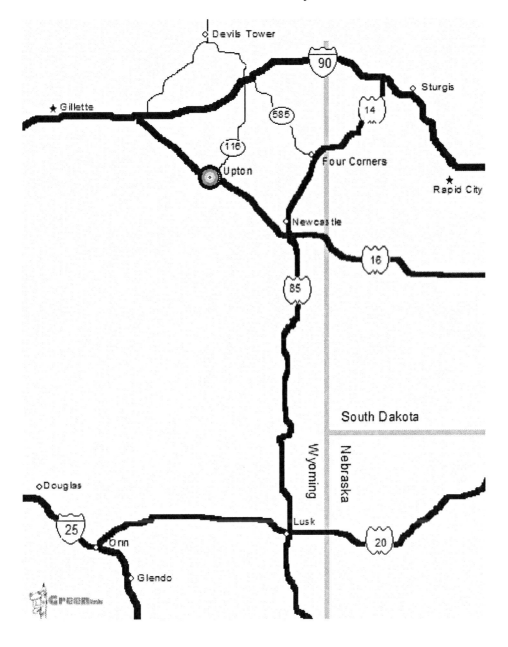

NAME: **L/C Bishop Sales**
LOCATION: 544 Circle Drive, Casper, WY 82601
TYPE: Indoor Range
COST: $3.00/ day
DIRECTIONS: From I-25 take N Poplar St south; turn west on W English Ave to the End; turn south on Circle Dr.
DESCRIPTION: Range is 6 lanes at 20 yards
CONTACT: Mike 307-235-1320

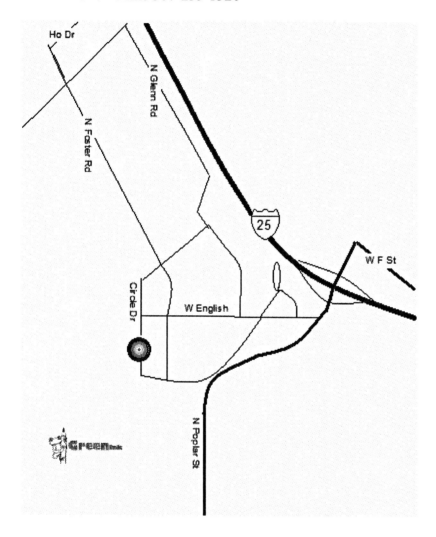

NAME: **Little Wind Archers of Fremont County**
LOCATION: 2125 East Monroe Ave. Riverton, WY 82501-4828
TYPE: Outdoor course and range, Indoor Range
COST: Memberships single $10.00, Family $15.00, and junior $8.00
DIRECTIONS: From Casper WY I25 take US-20 approx. 116 miles. Stay straight on S Federal Blvd for 0.3 miles. Turn Left on E Monroe Ave. for 0.7 miles.
DESCRIPTION: The Little Wind Archers of Fremont County is a not-for-profit social/recreational archery club located in Riverton, Wyoming which serves the entire Fremont County area as well as the rest of Wyoming. The Little Wind Archers are affiliated with the National Field Archery Association and the Wyoming State Archery Association. Our club's primary goal and purpose is to provide an opportunity for like-minded folks to engage in the recreational sport of archery, and to promote the sport of archery, target archery, 3-D archery as well as bow hunting to the Fremont County community at large. We welcome all archers and even non-archers to join with us, and participate in making our club a stronger partner in the Fremont County and Wyoming community.Our club schedules several 3-D archery tournaments every spring and summer, including two, 2-Day overnight foam hunting tournament excursions into the Shoshone National Forest. During the winter months we try to have an indoor target archery tournament or two. And every week from January to the end of April we schedule an informal archery league, where we compete against one another or just get together and practice our unique family sport.
CONTACT: Ron Reddon (307) 856-6651 littlewindarchers@yahoo.com
www.littlewindarchers.com

Illustration - Little Wind Archers of Fremont County

Little Wind Archers of Fremont County
2125 E Monroe Ave
Riverton WY
82501-4828

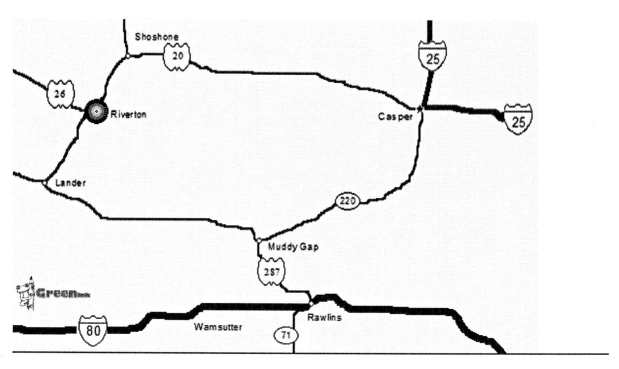

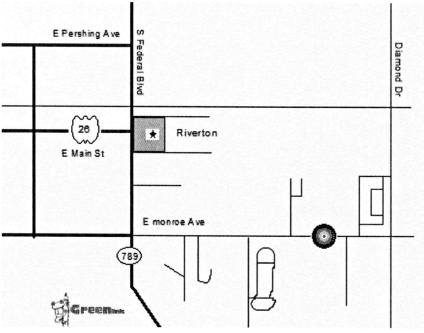

www.planetwildlife.net

NAME: **Lost Arrow Archers**
LOCATION: 1700 Fairgrounds Rd. Casper WY 82602-2919
TYPE: Indoor ranges – Outdoor ranges during summer months.
COST: $2 or $3 per night and $15 individual and $25 family for annuals
DESCRIPTION: Every Tuesday and Thursday they have 3-D shoots for $3 per individual. Every Sunday and Monday at the stuckdnoff shooters complex for $2. During summer months two 28 burlap target ranges with a animal figurines painted on them will be available with 15 ft. to 80 yard targets at the Robert L. Adams Memorial Archery Range on Casper mountain.

Robert L. Adams Memorial Archery Range is FREE for the public.
DIRECTIONS: From Casper take Casper Mountain Rd. South up the mountain. At the crest, archers will pass the Broken Spur Café. Veer right at the "Y" in the road – traveling on the road to Hogadon Ski Resort. ¼ mile before Hogadon archers will turn left on Micro Road, proceed approx. 1 mile, turning left before the small housing area. Travel approx. ¼ mile and turn right at the "T" in the road. Proceed 1 ½ miles to the archery range parking lot. 'The range is approx. 20 minutes from Casper.

Lost Arrow Archers of Casper Wyoming is a Not-for-Profit Recreational Archery Club. Our Club's primary goal and purpose is to provide an opportunity for people with similar interests to gather in the Sport of Archery, and to promote the sport of Target archery, 3-d Archery, as well as bow hunting in Central Wyoming. We WELCOME and encourage all Archers and non-archers to join with us, and participate in making our club a social and family oriented partner in Central Wyoming.

Lost Arrow Archers schedules several 3-D archery tournaments every Year, including a Triple Crown Event. In the summer a weekend Hunting/Competition event is scheduled on top of Casper Mountain at the Natrona County Archery Range. During the long winter Months we have archery league where everyone is invited to compete against one another or just come on out and get together and practice the sport of Archery.
CONTACT: Ken Thoren 307-237-1762 kthorend@admiralbeverage.com

Illustration Robert L. Adams Memorial Archery Range Entrance

Illustration Robert L. Adams Memorial Archery Range Point of View

Lost Arrow Archers
Casper WY

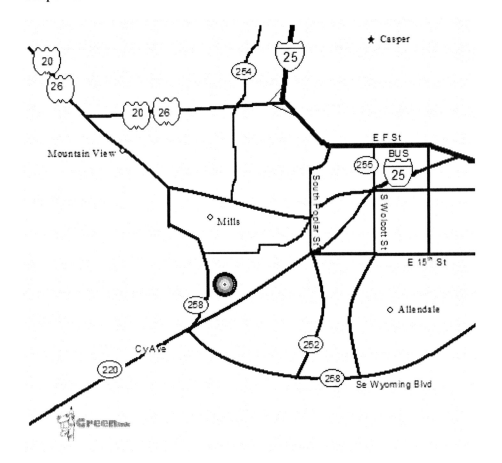

NAME: **Pronghorn Archery Club**
LOCATION: 4706 South Douglas Hwy, Gillette, WY 82718-6711
TYPE: Outdoor Range
COST: Annual Individual Membership $10.00; Family $15.00.
DIRECTIONS: End of Box Elder Road.
DESCRIPTION: 4 Lanes 15-80 yards.
CONTACT: Andy Turnquist 307-257-7509 http://pronghornarchery.homestead.com/

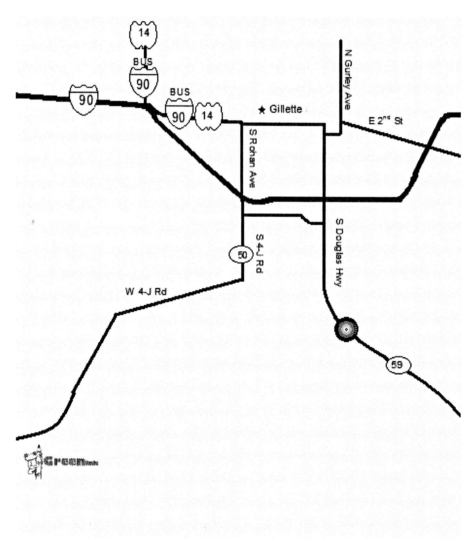

NAME: **Rocky Mountain Discount Sports**
LOCATION: 4706 S Douglas Hwy Gillette, WY 82718
TYPE: Indoor range
COST: Free
DIRECTIONS: From I90 take S Douglas Hwy (Hwy 59) approx. 2.2 miles.
DESCRIPTION: 10 lanes with techno hunt video screen
CONTACT: 307- 686-0221

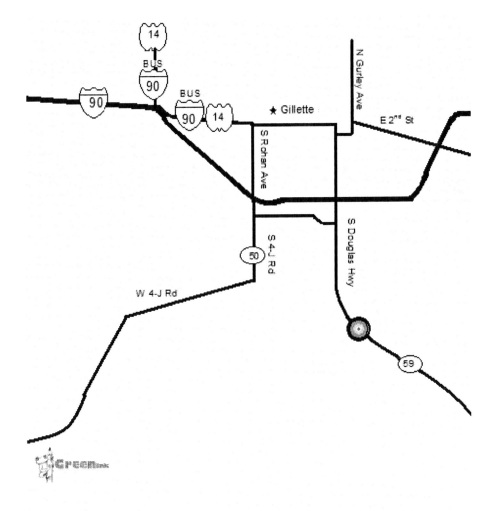

NAME: **Rocky Mountain Sports**
LOCATION: 1526 Rumsey Ave. Cody WY 82414-3871
TYPE: Indoor range and Dart System
COST: $3.00 per hour for Range and $10.00 per hour for Dart System
DIRECTIONS: Refer to maps.
DESCRIPTION: Target Range is 3 lanes at 20 yards and Dart System
CONTACT: 307- 527-6071

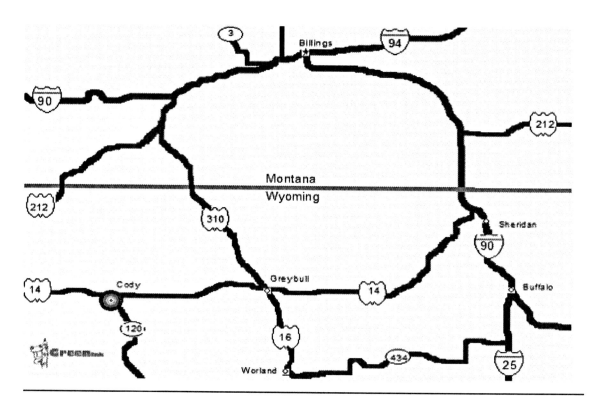

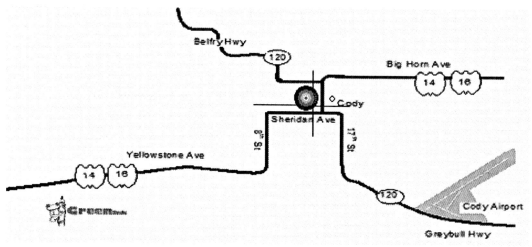

NAME: **White Mountain Archery**
LOCATION: P.O. Box 1258 Green River, WY 82935
TYPE: Indoor range
COST: $5.00 per day - $20 annual for a family - $55 for League Shoots
DIRECTIONS: Refer to map and call ahead for directions and schedule.
DESCRIPTION: Join in the fun of archery with this club! The group host regular shoots and tournaments. Practice Thu. Nights & Sat. Afternoons. 3-D on weekends: indoor during winter and outdoor from 10 to 100 yards in the summer.
CONTACT: Dwayne Palmer 307- 875-1950

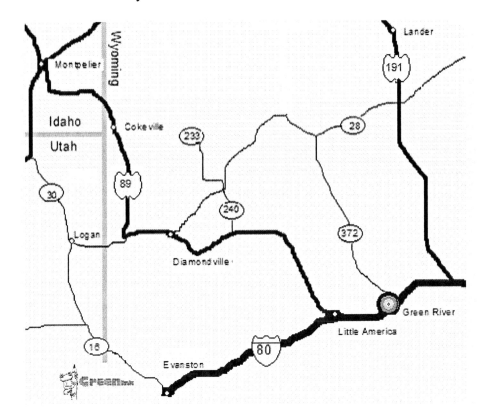

NAME: **Wyoming Archery & Hunting Supply**
LOCATION: 502 Coral St. Kemmerer, WY 83101
TYPE: Indoor range
COST: Free
DIRECTIONS: From I80 take US-30 North approx. 35 miles.
DESCRIPTION: Small range in basement of store.
CONTACT: 307-877-2917

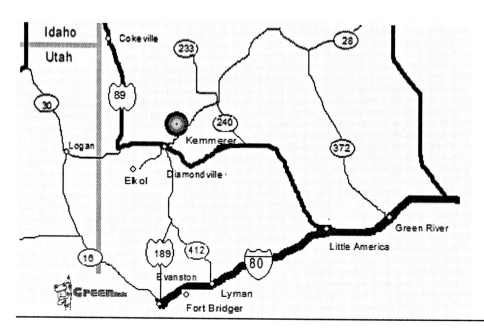

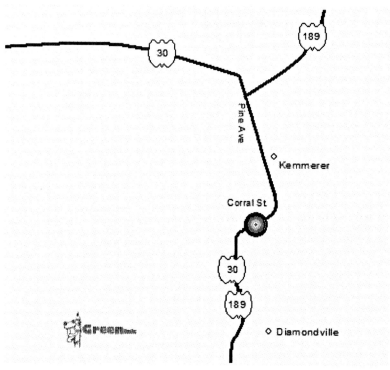

About the publisher.

Planet wildlife is a group dedicated to the preservation and proliferation of wildlife on our planet. All profits from book sales are donated to wildlife charities, state and national parks. All profits from this book, our first in a national series, will be donated to wild sage grouse population programs.

Planet wildlife is the leading specialist in wildlife safaris. Check out our website for upcoming events or reserve your own custom base-camp today. Your ncxt hunting trip could be a safari!

Stuff

Books

Guide to Rocky Mountain Archery Courses and Ranges Volume
I...........................$19.95
Available on CD.............................$24.95

Guide to Rocky Mountain Archery Courses and Ranges Volume
II...........................$19.95
Available on CD.............................$24.95

Guide to Backcountry Snowboarding in the Rocky
Mountains...................................$19.95
Available on CD.............................$24.95

Safari Cooking for lovers....................$19.95
Available on CD.............................$24.95

Guide to Backcountry Cross Country Skiing/Snow Shoeing in the Rocky
Mountains.........$19.95
Available on CD.............................$24.95

Rocky Mountain Survival Guide...........$19.95
Available on CD.............................$24.95

Archery Exercises for balance and spinal alignment
....$19.95
Available on CD.............................$24.95

DVD's

Camp Cooking made Easy....................$24.95

Archery Exercise for Balance................$24.95

Girls Survival Guide to Camping.............$24.95

Pit Barbeque $24.95

Safari Setup $24.95

Camping with Man's Best Friend............$24.95

Products

Survival Pack- Full Car size...................$199.95

Survival Pack –Medium Backpack size.....$99.95

Survival Pack –City purse sized..............$79.95

Archery Exercise Kit...........................$349.95

Comments

Please add me to your mailing list.

Name: _____

Address: _____

_____

Please add the following business or club to your next edition:

NAME: _____

LOCATION: _____

_____

TYPE: _____

COST: _____

DESCRIPTION: _____

_____

_____

CONTACT: _____

_____

General Remarks or Suggestions:

_____

_____

_____

_____

_____

Planet Wildlife
1200 W 22nd Street
Cheyenne WY 82001-3429

Index

Sponsors

Planet Wildlife would like to extend special thanks to the following contributors for their generous donations. Their support in getting this book to final publication is a credit to humanity and their concern for our nation's wildlife.

Special Thanks to:

Green Inc.; for most of the maps found in this publication and book cover design.
www.greeninkcomics.com

Magic Dragons House; for on location filming.
www.magicdragonshouse.com

Midnight Tourist; for providing location planning and catoring.
www.midnighttourist.com

Mr. Big Bad; for providing custom string silencers and safety equipment.
www.mrbigbad.com

Liberty Archery; for their donation of one Liberty I bow with accessories.
www.libertyarchery.com

KGWN Channel 5 News in Cheyenne WY; for free television promotional air time.
www.kgwn.tv

KGAB Radio 650 AM in Cheyenne WY; for free promotional radio air time.
www.kgab.com/main.php

KOLZ radio 100.7 FM in Cheyenne WY ; for free promotional radio air time.
www.koltfm.com/main.html

KING Radio 101.9 FM in Cheyenne WY; for free promotional radio air time.
www.kingfm.com/main.php

MY NOTES

States included:

Idaho
Montana
Utah
Wyoming
Colorado
Arizona
New Mexico

106 Entries.

1st Edition
First printing
December 2007

Planet wildlife press
1201 W 22nd Street
Cheyenne, WY 82001

USD $19.95